What Others Are Saying

"Dr. Lamar Vest, in *Faith to Stand When You Can't Understand,* is righteously impatient with a view of faith that offers superficial answers to life's vital questions, misrepresents the gospel, and may ultimately lead people away from following Christ. He describes erroneous portrayals of the gospel and provides a biblical, thoughtful, and practical perspective on true faith, rooted in theological certainty and enriched by his personal experiences. This book will help people whose spiritual questions remain unanswered find a foundation for faith."

> Mark L. Williams
> Presiding Bishop/General Overseer
> Church of God

"I have known Lamar Vest for forty years. I have watched him undergo what it means and costs to truly love God, his family, friends, church and neighbors of all walks of life around the world. Deeply rooted in his faith tradition and experience, he is globally connected. Ours has been a dialog of a costly relationship in which we have grieved, rejoiced and worked together. He has been my friend, brother, leader, student, teacher and colleague.

His authenticity comes through in *Faith to Stand When You Can't Understand,* and it will draw you in. The more you have endured in your life, the more you will sense the divine comfort in this printed means of grace. (2 Corinthians 1:3-5) Lamar Vest is a good man who longs to see faith fully formed and rooted in the sons and daughters of future generations so they will care deeply, love faithfully and stand with unwavering trust in God."

> Dr. Steven J. Land
> President, Pentecostal Theological Seminary

"Dr. Lamar Vest has distinguished himself as a world leader, but the rich experiences, as well as endurance of life, has given him an uncommon wisdom and character. He imparts this wisdom unselfishly in his book, **Faith to Stand**. His keen insight is filled with timeless principles for life. Each chapter leaves you wanting more."

> Dr. Bryan Cutshall
> St. Louis, Missouri

"Lamar Vest has perceptibly discerned the need of the day and powerfully communicates that confident living in Christ will overcome circumstances and the work of the enemy. He passionately offers encouragement to all of us whose faith is challenged."

> Dan Busby
> President, ECFA

"I have seen Lamar Vest in the most trying of leadership circumstances. His capacious, but centered faith was revealed in his actions and is now described in this poignant chronicle of his Christian journey. Persons across the religious spectrum will find in this volume instructions for living a life of Christian integrity and guidance for a courageous and confident confrontation with life's uncertainties. Whatever the results, one will always find a loving and sovereign God who loves and accepts us just as we are. Lamar Vest testifies to these eternal truths throughout the pages of this book."

> Dennis C. Dickerson
> James M. Lawson, Jr. Professor of History
> Vanderbilt University

"As I began reading, **Faith to Stand** today at 5:00 am, I became aware that I've been living somewhere between faith and trust since my son, David, went to be with the Lord three years ago. David had said to me, "Dad, it will be difficult, but it will be okay". With my son's last breath on that night, my faith leaped from faith to trust in the Sovereign Lord. It was not until I read this book, that the "Sovereign Okay" part of David's statement became a reality for me. I didn't understand it, but now it's much clearer. To be reminded that I have journeyed where all of us have journeyed, makes me understand that I'm not alone.

Every person who has the guts to read and seriously consider the implications of this book could be relieved, renewed and redeemed from the mediocrity of cliché Christian communication. I know I will never be the same."
> Dr. Tony Capps
> President/Founder
> InVision Solutions, Inc.

"Over the years that I've had the privilege of knowing Dr. Lamar Vest, I have learned that he is a man of genuine and steadfast faith in the gospel of Christ. Not only in his capacity as the former President of American Bible Society, but also in his own personal walk, Dr. Vest desires to understand the truth of God's word more fully, and to put it into practice. This book demonstrates his devotion to seeking the Person of God – not just symbolism or religious constructs – and to walking more closely with Him every day. Through this practical and sincere reflection on his own experiences, Dr. Vest cuts to the heart of the modern struggle to build our faith on a real relationship with Christ, rather than on the symbols, rituals, or cultural constructs of religion. Refreshingly, he urges us not to hide our doubts and questions, or to suppress our boldest inquiries about who God is. He urges us to openly bring our inquiries about truth both to the foot of the cross and the throne of heaven. I applaud him for his candor on such a critically important subject, and I thank him for challenging the faith community in the United States. His book is written precisely for such a time as this. We would do well to heed his sound words of counsel."
> The Reverend Luis Cortés, Jr.
> President, Esperanza

This book is prayerfully and joyfully dedicated to the truthful people in my life. Those who have not been afraid to confront me with the truth, in love, and challenge me to live up to the high expectations of one who is called out of darkness into His marvelous light.

They know who they are.
Thank you!

Faith to Stand When You Can't Understand

When Life Hurts and Answers Aren't Enough

Lamar Vest

MINDSHIFT PUBLISHING, DBA STEVEN LESTER

ATLANTA, GEORGIA

Contents

Foreword

L amar Vest is a father to the church.

Paul wrote clearly of the power and God's ordained purpose of this role in his letter to the Corinthian believers.

I write not these things to shame you, but as my beloved sons I warn you.

For though ye have ten thousand instructors in Christ, yet have ye not many fathers:

for in Christ Jesus I have begotten you through the gospel.

Wherefore I beseech you, be ye followers of me.

I Corinthians 4:14-16

We live in an age where many voices, though often sincere, have led countless followers of Jesus Christ into confusion. Between the bookends of unguided optimism to deliberate deception, scores now stand at a crossroad of wondering if the Messiah they have trusted in is, in fact, trustworthy.

Opinions abound, but the voice of a father overpowers them all. A father speaks with authority and calm assurance. Having had the experience of flood and fire, he can speak of that which stands when all else has failed. It is the one and final voice that says "… This is the way, walk ye in it" (Isaiah 30:21).

Lamar Vest has been given such a voice. He has been led of the Lord into a place where the self-appointed cannot go.

Indeed in our generation there have been many teachers. Though thankful for some of what has been taught, I as well as you need the father's voice to navigate the troubled days in which we live.

I highly recommend this book. In it Lamar Vest does not speak for God, rather God through him speaks for Himself.

Pastor Carter Conlon
Senior Pastor
Times Square Church
Manhattan, NYC

Preface

Perfect people will not understand nor perhaps even value this book. But that's okay. It actually isn't written for them. It's for the rest of us. It is for those who have not always lived on the mountaintops of ecstasy but have spent some time in the valley of uncertainty. It is for those who don't have answers to all the questions and know it. It is for those who do not view the Christian life as a place of instant "arrival" but more as a journey toward a confident, unmovable relationship with Jesus Christ.

There was a time in my life when I thought I had arrived. I felt as though I was immune to questions or doubts. But several incidents, most of which are still too personal and too painful to commit to writing, came rushing in, shook me at the very core of the foundation where I stood and dragged me off my pedestal of certainty.

I have come to terms with the understanding that my faith in God does not depend upon my having all the answers. I am confidently standing in the belief that God does not place upon human beings a requirement to know and understand everything about God and faith. Believing, at least for me, is a process rather than a position at which I have arrived.

For me, the Christian life is a journey which has led to the mountains of triumph and to the wilderness of distress. It has led through the sunshine and the rain, through joy and sorrow. But it has always led me closer to God. Someone has rightly said, *'The will of God will never lead you where the grace of God cannot keep you.'*

I have wanted to write about these issues for a long time, but I think I have been reluctant to open this faucet. Afraid, I suppose, that too much may come pouring out and also perhaps fearful that I might be unable to adequately explain what I am feeling. But, I'm now willing to risk these possible consequences for my own sake and, hopefully, for the sake of others who may identify with something I share. I have a feeling there are those who have heard all of the pretentious religious clichés and have struggled in an effort to reconcile them with personal experiences and with their understanding of the Word. I strongly suspect that many still wrestle with questions of divine providence and the superficiality of some of the classical platitudes that have become part of our Christian vernacular. I have personally had to help pick up the pieces of those shattered by the reality that the "truisms," those trite and overused expressions about religion which are often mouthed without thought or Scriptural foundation, aren't always true and are seldom satisfying.

This book is not written as a mere theological or theoretical treatise nor primarily as an evangelistic appeal. My hope is to confront some of those gnawing questions which emerge ever so often in the lives of those who are well into their journey of faith.

This is a book about confident trust when circumstances

become overwhelming. It's about finding the faith to stand when your foundations are shaken, when your life is hurt deeply, and the answers you are given do not satisfy your questions. The words confidence and trust are, as used in Scripture, virtually the same thing. Whenever trust in God is mentioned in Scripture, it means to have confidence. Faith is all about a deep-seated confidence in God and is reflected in how we live our lives. By definition, confidence is truth that is reliable and trustworthy.

> **It's about finding the faith to stand when your foundations are shaken, when your life is hurt deeply, and the answers you are given do not satisfy your questions.**

I am also hopeful this book will influence some young leader who is standing at a door of decision in how to minister to someone who is confronted with a catastrophic event. It is my prayer that you will be able to honestly reflect on the questions that haunt so many in our churches, our nation, and in our culture of how to have faith to stand even when you cannot understand the why of a situation. When our own life hurts so deeply and the question resounds within our hearts *'Can we really trust God?'* we often realize that some of the answers we've heard or even spoken ourselves are not enough.

When life becomes "just too much," we may find ourselves struggling with previously concealed stresses which all seem to pile up at once. Confidence is a funny thing. When you have it, you can face almost anything. When you lose it, it seems you can't even face going out of your front door. We can feel destabilized because our rule has broken down. We can begin to question whether we are truly competent and worthy, and maybe even question our position with God. Suddenly our confidence is gone. We no longer take risks, and may avoid things that we once could do quite easily. The world suddenly seems a vast and scary place.

Confidence has to be backed up by honesty and consistency. From the human perspective, to be a person of confidence means that we must say what we're going to do and then do what we said we were going to do.

Deep within our hearts, we suspect that we cannot always trust others to live up to their promises and are certain we can't always trust our own feelings. Our consistency and the consistency of others are not the issue. The issue is *'Can we always trust God?'* When you don't understand the circumstances of life and your confidence is depleted, how can you find the faith to stand? That's the question upon which our entire faith rests, and it is the question I wish to address in the following pages.

Christ-living is a state of being that releases us from the bondage of circumstances and opens us to the wonderful reality that the truth of God will always prevail. Confident Christian living is distinguished by an ever-increasing confidence that God is more than equal to personal or cultural brokenness. Confident Christian living realizes that wilderness experiences are not merely detours on life's journey, but are battlegrounds that Christ uses to prepare and transform us for the here and now and for the hereafter. Today's tests become tomorrow's testimonies.

The truth is that we are *all* pilgrims on this path of life, often having to chop away at the brush and overgrowth of superficial substance to find our way. We are missionaries, not wayfarers. We are disciples, not weekend tourists. None of us have arrived. We are all in the process of becoming. We are all still following in the footsteps of the Master. No one has all the answers to all the questions for one simple reason. To have reached that status would place us on the same level with God, Who alone knows and understands all things.

My passion is to share what I feel God has placed in my heart, often by way of personal struggles. All I am responsible for is merely writing it down, however crude my skills of communication may be. The outcome is up to God.

If the following pages sometimes lapse into the powerfully, roaring expressions of a Sunday sermon, I trust no harm will be done. It is merely the passionate heart-cry of one who has already traveled this path before. I don't mean to shout at you, and I'm certainly not necessarily trying to instruct you. I suppose I feel more as C. S. Lewis has said, *"People need more to be reminded than to be instructed."*

Lamar Vest

Introduction

It was the end of a hectic day. I made my way to my seat at the very back of the airplane, hoping for some quiet time of reflection about the meeting I had just left.

The overhead compartments were all full, and there was no room to place my luggage under the seat in front of me. The flight attendant informed me that I would have to check my carry-on bag, which was something I did not want to do. I thought about putting up a stiff protest, but quickly overcame this impulse and replied, *"Well, if I have to, but I really prefer to keep it with me."* I followed up with a joke to *clarify* my concern, *"For me, there are only two kinds of luggage, carry on and lost."*

The man assigned to the seat beside me apparently took notice of my attempt at humor and suggested that my bag would fit under the seat in front of the one assigned to him. I thanked him and sat down.

I didn't want to talk, but I felt some obligation since he had been so accommodating. When I noticed that he was holding a copy of "The Book," a Living Bible Translation of Scripture, I felt an even stronger responsibility to say something. *"Does that book help you?"* I inquired, tongue-in-cheek, assuming that since he was unashamed to produce a Bible on a crowded airplane, he must be a devoted believer.

"I hope the h_ _ _ it can," he replied. *"I haven't read it in a while, but my life is in such shambles I picked it up again and decided to give it another chance. I used to believe it and follow it, but my religion stopped working for me."*

That statement went right to my heart; *"my religion stopped working for me."* I knew right away that I was going to be engaged in conversation for the entire flight. In the course of the conversation, I learned that things had failed to work out in this man's life as his pastor and some of his church friends had promised, so he simply gave up. He readily produced another book from his briefcase written by a prominent minister-and-wife team which, he said, had promised that true believers never had to worry about facing discouragement and failure. He had read it… and believed it … and it had worked for awhile. When it stopped working, he stopped believing. Because things had gotten even worse, he decided to give religion one more try out of desperation. This time, however, he was searching for a new formula. He looked at me and asked, *"Do you have any ideas?"*

My memory exploded with my own disappointments regarding the malfunction of religious formulas that had proven woefully inadequate…

My memory exploded with several of my own disappointments regarding the malfunction of religious formulas that had proven woefully inadequate for my circumstances. I wasn't about to bog him down with further exploration of religious clichés. He had already had enough of them. *"If there is such a formula,"* I said, *"I haven't found it."* My suggestion to him was that he should give up trying to find a religion that would work in life's circumstances and to begin to learn the meaning of confidence in God Who is greater than any circumstance.

"It seems to me," I said, *"that it is time for you to do some trusting."* *"For me,"* I added, *"when I have doubts, I know it is time to put a new edge on my relationship with God, not in symbols and formulas."*

As I later reflected on that incident, I realized that although most people do not express it in such transparent, graphic terms, his dilemma was not an uncommon occurrence. In fact, many casualties of the Christian faith can be traced back to the point where someone felt they had all the answers and had allowed themselves to settle into the comfort zone of ceremonial religion. Among the most dangerous heresies to weaken the Christian church is an error which emerged in the first century and has surfaced in every generation since. It is the error which attempts to delude people with the idea that right form, right doctrine, and right ritual constitute the whole of Christianity. There are those who have mistakenly concluded that all that is necessary for successful Christian living is to say the right words, sing the right choruses, or reach the plateau of continual, joyous ecstasy. People often tend to turn to religion more out of an effort to find ways to improve their own circumstances rather than to establish a right relationship with God.

Influenced by colloquial and personalized beliefs, many view Christianity as a system of accomplishments which, if mastered, will deliver desired results. They view the Christian life as a performance model, involving constant self-examination and standardized tests. They view Christianity only as providing benefits in the here-and-now and for the hereafter, and have concluded that it's a pretty good deal after all. If, however, we serve Christ and minister to the needs of others only because of the benefits derived, we are essentially attempting to serve ourselves through them. It could be seen as using Jesus and others to get what we want. This approach to Christianity profanes the Gospel of Jesus Christ. It takes that which is holy and reduces it to the level of magic and mythology.

Too many people today have reduced the Christian life to a few formulas for ease of communication. Marketing techniques that attempt to reduce Christianity to a few poignant sound bites may be suitable for a thirty-second commercial, but will never be sufficient for a culture searching for Truth. It is vital to confident Christian living that we draw our understanding of the whole Gospel from the whole Bible and allow God's Spirit to draw our story into the story of Scripture.

I am amazed at how many books attempt to utilize secular principles for Biblical causes. There are five-step, seven-step, or twelve-step plans to receive anything you want or go anywhere you want, that is, except to a rightful relationship with God. People want God's principles without God. It doesn't work that way. You can't have the principles without the Person.

Principles themselves have no redeeming or transforming power. What the human race needs is the purpose and principles incarnated in the Person of Jesus Christ. No formula or set of principles can furnish this. Jesus called men and women away from an external and formalistic religion to an inward and personal faith, one of personal fellowship. As Joseph M. Stowell has said, "Christ brought religion on God's terms and the self-styled religionists of His day, the Pharisees and the Sadducees, ultimately killed Him. True religion is intolerable in a false religious system" (Joseph M. Stowell, *Through The Fire,* (Wheaton, Illinois: Victor Books, 1985) p. 58).

Paul says in Galatians 2:20, "I have been crucified with Christ; it is no longer I who live, but Christ lives in me; and the life which I now live in the flesh I live by faith in the Son of God, who loved me and gave Himself for me" (NKJ). Here Paul tells us that we are *not* going to be judged by performance. He directed us away from any false hope that our own performance will glorify God. Paul was saying there is another way. He knew that our only hope for success lay within the bounds of our union with Christ.

The metaphors that Paul uses are graphic and somewhat startling. He says, "I am crucified." Capture that image if you can. I am on a cross. I am naked before my accusers. Soldiers are beneath me gambling for my possessions. There are nails in my hands and feet. I am crowned with thorns. I am crucified. I am dead.

This is not the typical picture of success, is it? But, to be successful in Christian living, I have to realize that I am dead in terms of my performance making me right with God. All of my being, all of my doing, all of my positions, all of my trophies mean nothing in terms of my standing with God.

This is the potent antidote for spiritual pride. On the cross, achievement dies because the performance standard is dead. I can no longer boast that I am better than you, wiser than you, or more important than you. If we are Christ's, we are all dead. This is not only the antidote for spiritual pride, but it is also the antidote for spiritual despair. All the things that traditionally separate Christians from one another are crucified on the cross. All my failures, all my shortcomings, all my shame of the past, are all dead. All nailed to the cross.

But there is something else in its place. Christ lives in me! That is much more than a statement that Christ energizes me. It is more than a warm, fuzzy feeling. I am dead as far as this world is concerned! He is alive! He lives in me.

All of His wisdom. All His concern for the lost and the suffering. All His righteousness. All of that is mine, because He lives in me. All that is Christ's, is mine. That's why Paul could say, "For me to live is Christ." So many people are in such a mess today, because they believe they are worthless or they feel they can't quite measure up. If you feel that you are worthless, then you are helpless. Christ proved your worth by dying on a cross for you. His living through you underscores your extreme value to Him.

There are some Christians who actually seem to prefer surrendering their souls to legalistic rules, regulations, agendas, principles or formulas rather than choosing to live in harmony with Jesus Christ. They strain and sweat through spiritual exercises as if these activities were designed to transform them into a super-Christian. God is repelled by all the formulas we create. Paul emphasizes that the Christian life is much more than rituals and formulas. He insists that the "... mysteries of God are in Christ, in whom are hid all the treasures of wisdom and knowledge" (Colossians 2:2-3, KJV). In other words, all we have is because of Christ, not because of anything we do. Our greatest goal is to know Him.

If we, in fact, believe that God appoints circumstances to change and conform us to His image, we should stop fighting to avoid everything and anything disconcerting that comes our way. Instead, we should embrace them and pray for understanding so that we may grow spiritually and benefit from what God has allowed to happen.

Coming to Christ does not remove nor exempt us from the trials of human existence.

Coming to Christ does not remove nor exempt us from the trials of human existence, and, personally, I am glad it doesn't. When I look back over my life, it seems that my most endearing and cherished experiences in the Christian life have emerged from the crucibles of some extremely difficult situations. The Christian faith, at least for me, is the belief that God is *worthy* of being trusted, in spite of my circumstances. It is a matter of confidence. When life hurts and simple answers aren't enough, you must develop a faith to stand in spite of all the things that you cannot understand in the moment. Belief doesn't become *faith* until we have enough confidence to believe that God can be trusted completely, always and in all situations.

I have found that the one element common to successful Christian living is persistence. The Apostle James said in James 1:4,

"Perseverance must finish its work so that you may be mature and complete, not lacking anything" (NIV). You've got to hang in there, especially when the demons of doubt gang up to challenge whatever spark of faith you have left. You've got to reach that level of confident living where you know that your circumstances, regardless of how intimidating they may seem, will not prevail. But your trust in God will.

At some point in each of our lives, we will struggle with perceived inconsistencies between our experiences and in what the Bible says. If left unaddressed, these apparent discrepancies can deal a staggering blow to faith. Although our experiences do not add revelation to the Bible, to assume those experiences or circumstances don't exist is not facing reality. We must continue to address the *'Is this really true?'* question.

For years, I have been concerned that many Christians have what I call a "frantic faith." This faith has to be worked up by frenzied exertion or bolstered by qualifying factors. Others seem to have an *'I hope I'm right by trusting in God, but I'll have to wait and see'* attitude. I long to see believers gripped with a calm assurance that human circumstances, human failures and human resourcefulness will never impede the settled plan of God.

If you wish to use your faith only as a formula for having all of your needs met, chances are you will live your life in constant frustration. The question is not whether or not your religion works. The question is, *'Is God faithful and does He warrant your absolute trust in Him?'*

the Failure of False Assumptions

Three neighborhood boys who were brothers watched intently as the massive truck drove into the vacant lot next to the textile mill. They knew something was up. They just didn't know exactly what. Clearly, this was unusual activity for their drowsy, little mill village, and they sure didn't want to miss out on it.

With concealed interest, the boys strolled close enough to see if they could hear the conversation between the two men who had gotten out of the truck.

"We can pitch the big top right about there," grunted the brawny man in overalls, pointing to a spot in the center of the vacant lot.

"Hear that, don't you?" asked the oldest boy. *"They're gonna pitch a tent here. And you know what that means? A circus is coming town."*

The youngest of the three brothers mumbled, *"Wish I could go to a circus! I've never been to a circus in all of my life."*

"Well, you're not gonna get to go to this one either," retorted the

third boy. *"You know daddy's not gonna give us the money to go to the circus!"* he said, as if to put an end to all their hopeful excitement.

"Maybe we don't have to have money," said the oldest. *"The way I figure it, we can hide in the bushes on the back side and slip under the tent once it's dark. Nobody will ever see us."* And that's exactly what they did.

But, there was a slight problem. The boys were to be shocked later that night by what they learned when they sneaked in and sat down in the big tent. It was a circus tent all right, but what was going on inside the tent was not at all what they had expected. As they slid under the tent flap, they found themselves right in the middle of an old-fashioned Gospel revival service. Imagine their disappointment when their excitement was squelched by a 'bait and switch' ploy in their expectations.

From what I've observed recently, I believe there are a great number of Christians who can identify with these boys. It seems that many are being attracted to the church and the Christian message because someone preached to them a gospel that promises a life of complete health, wealth and happiness. The problem is that once they get in and discover that their religion doesn't live up to its advertisement, they become disillusioned.

To many people, religion has become a human thing. It is religion which has attempted to remake God into man's image. It is religion which assumes that God's Voice has become the echo of man's voice. For many, religion has become the magic potion that can be applied to all of life's situations. Magic promises results. One such promise of this kind of religion is that if you employ the tried and proven principles, you will get the guaranteed outcome. But, what do we do when, as Walter Brueggemann has said, "God refuses to be useful" (Walter Bruggerman, *Hopeful Imagination*, (Philadelphia: Fortress Press, 1986) p. 7).

To produce any experience through human management makes that experience something less than Christian.

To produce any experience through human management makes that experience something less than Christian. Thus, any attempt to influence or coerce individuals to become a Christian by any means other than those which are clearly established in the Gospel makes the proponent a false prophet.

Imagine the shock of some church-goers who think they are slipping into an arena of fun, frolic, and fantasy when they suddenly discover they are smack in the middle of a spiritual war which may cost them their lives. Think of the disappointments experienced by those who have been told that a just God will not allow the righteous to suffer, but they find themselves right in the middle of a raging trial. That may be a hint as to why some Christians have retreated quietly into a place of protected isolation, apparently disillusioned or, at least, disappointed with their religion, yet too embarrassed to admit it. Disappointment is the forerunner of estrangement from one's faith.

Although disappointment with God may not be the acknowledged behavior for Christians, chances are you know many Christians who harbor deeply-buried disappointments within their hearts. Embarrassment or fear almost always prohibits persons from expressing their disappointments loudly enough to be heard, yet, we all know they are there.

Embarrassment or fear almost always prohibits persons from expressing their disappointments loudly enough to be heard, yet, we all know they are there.

Not all disappointed Christians totally give up their faith immediately. They often hold on to the ceremony while convictions silently lapse into a semi-comatose state of sentimentality. Confident trust gives way to uncertainty. Calm assurance is replaced by frenzied activity. Devotion succumbs to duty. The inevitable result is to pose as a great pretender and live as though everything is okay.

Some time ago, I heard of a man in one of the New England states who kept a personal secret for many years. No one suspected that anything was wrong. Even at home, among family, his behavior appeared normal. Every night after dinner he would sit in his favorite recliner with the newspaper. Not even his wife was aware of his problem.

Finally, the day came when he could no longer keep up the masquerade. After many years of guarding his secret, he finally confessed that he was unable to read. He had been living a life of pretense.

Too many Christians feel compelled to put up a front or a kind of mask. Even though the pretentious front might begin in a self-protective effort to shield an inadequacy, it soon drifts toward something much worse. This seemingly harmless attitude of some Christians to self-protect begins to lead to the compulsion of projecting the right language and constantly making a good impression.

Some people may consider these pretenders to be model Christians. However, deep inside, these individuals know that it is all make-believe. They often wrestle through the night with their contradictions and the gnawing fears of being found out. Sadly, in the light of day, fear and uncertainty almost always cause some to default to the perceived security of formulas, rituals, and clichés rather than true confidence and integrity of faith. This often leads to a search for the latest *success techniques* in order to overcome lingering fear and pretentious posturing.

A hurting soul is seen by some as evidence of spiritual immaturity or some heretical malady. That's probably why we Christians learn early how to pretend that we feel okay when we know deep inside that we feel anything but okay. We seem surrounded by a conspiracy of pretense. In all reality, a hurting soul is probably evidence of a simple case of realism. As long as we are on this present earth, there is no way to escape the pain and suffering common to all humanity.

It seems that a modern version of Christianity with its gospel of always perfect health, wealth and happiness is all about escaping the experience of sorrow and lament. We are encouraged to skip right over any call to endure suffering and get right to the benefits. That is precisely the opposite of what our Lord taught!

Jesus said, John 16:33, "I have told you these things, so that in Me you may have [perfect] peace and confidence. In the world you have tribulation and trials and distress and frustration; but be of good cheer [take courage; be confident, certain, undaunted]! For I have overcome the world. [I have deprived it of power to harm you and have conquered it for you]" (AMP).

Paul says in Romans 8:18, "For I consider that the sufferings of this present time [this present life] are not worth being compared with the glory that is about to be revealed to us and in us and for us and conferred on us" (AMP).

New ideas about God and Christianity are flying over our heads like clouds on a windy day. When listening to some TV preachers, you may get the idea they have achieved fame and success, because they have perfected a foolproof formula that is available to anyone who will do as they say. They use bits and pieces of the Word to support their chosen formulas. God is used as only one element of their formulas. These *merchants of technique* seem to guarantee results if you have faith and will follow their formula. Naturally, if you don't get what you want, these purveyors of half-truth would imply, it must be your fault. You, obviously, didn't have enough faith.

A.W. Tozer warned, "Today, much of the church has gone in for theatrics, running a showboat instead of a lifeboat; staging a performance instead of an experience; having a form of godliness without the power thereof." Increasingly, people are being repulsed by the theatrics of religion. All you have to do is flip the channel, and you'll find someone espousing a similar formula to sell real estate, to help you find the love of your life, or enhance your memory.

Obviously, many innocent people are being misled, and that is tragic. *'But they are innocent,'* you say, *'and God won't hold them responsible.'* Innocent or not, those who buy into false religion pay the consequences. Imagine you are in a restaurant and someone gives you a counterfeit hundred-dollar bill to pay your check. Guess what? You are going to be the one to suffer the consequences when you give that fake money to the cashier. The person who gave you the counterfeit bill is long gone, but you are left with the consequences of either washing dishes, or, even worse, having the police called. Despite your innocence, it is you who suffers.

Some of the newly-developed ideas about Christianity definitely present problems. If indeed, the Christian faith means that you are able to get from God anything for which you ask, how do you respond when it seems that God has totally ignored something which is absolutely vital to you? How do you feel when you presume that God has answered a similar prayer for someone else, and it was a prayer you doubt was prayed any more sincerely and with any more faith than that with which you prayed? Does it mean you didn't have enough faith? Then, how much is enough?

Does it take *more* faith to have a prayer answered or be healed than it does to experience salvation? If so, how do I know when I've had enough faith to accept salvation? Faith is not a commodity to be measured in the capacities we often use.

Jesus said in Matthew 17:20, "Because of your unbelief; for assuredly, I say to you, if you have faith as a mustard seed, you will say to this mountain, 'Move from here to there,' and it will move; and nothing will be impossible for you" (NKJV). A tiny mustard seed of faith is *mountain-moving.* Yet, faith immeasurable, resulting in a great miraculous event, is not the primary lesson to be learned through these Scriptures.

Jesus is telling His disciples that nothing God asks them to do will be impossible if they trust Him. Moving this mountain is more about placing total confidence in God and no longer yielding to fearful or apparently unmovable circumstances. Trusting God to do what is good for you–and those around you–means that your circumstances no longer control your life.

Trusting in God is the only hope to live by in this life. Yet, when trusting God, we find that relationship with Him cannot be exhaustively understood in human definition and understanding. Isaiah 55:8-9 reminds us of this understanding, "For my thoughts are not your thoughts, neither are my ways, saith the Lord. For as the heavens are higher than the earth, so are my ways higher than your ways, and my thoughts than your thoughts."

Some actions or non-actions of God are, and always will be, beyond our limited understanding.

Some actions or non-actions of God are, and always will be, beyond our limited understanding. It is important to be reminded that God is not withholding crucial life-answers as someone who plays a guessing game with his children! We are unable to fully comprehend His thoughts or exhaustively understand how He chooses to orchestrate transformational, holy plans in our lives. Dr. Ravi Zacharias said, "God has put enough into the world to make faith in Him a most reasonable thing. But He has left enough out to make it impossible to live by sheer reason or observation alone"

(Ravi Zacharias International Ministries, www.rzim.org).

Christianity was never intended to be offered as a simple solution or as the standardized answer to any personal anguish. Jesus is not a medication to be taken on an as needed basis or a commodity to be purveyed. The Bible is not a book of holy riddles. It is not a fetish to drive off evil and bring on good. It never claims to be merely a textbook of science, literature or history. It is a revelation of God's desire for a relationship with His people. It is God's story delivered to you through the birth, life, suffering, death and resurrection of His Son.

Joseph M. Stowell has observed that "Mankind has an insatiable appetite for religion, but we fashion God according to ourselves. We recreate and distort Him into the form of our own tastes. In the process, His justice, righteousness, wrath, and holiness are lost. He becomes less than sovereign. His Word is not authoritative, but rather an assemblage of fascinating tales to be applied in a convenient, nonthreatening way" (Joseph M. Stowell, *Through The Fire*, (Wheaton, Illinois: Victor Books, 1985) p. 58).

Unfortunately, there is quite a bit of false advertisement regarding Christianity. It doesn't come from the Bible but from overly-anxious defenders who have adopted a "whatever it takes" practicality approach to Christianity. The problem is that no person has yet to build a correct life on a false conception. Taking partial truth for the whole truth leads to fanaticism. True believers must stay persistently in the Presence of the God of the Word.

Chapter 1

The Enticement of Post-Modern Religion

It's no wonder that some people are so perplexed about Christianity. It's confusing when they hear that Christians are meant to always be happy, because they know *they* don't always feel happy. They hear that Christians are meant to be fulfilled all the time, and yet *they* are not fulfilled. They hear that if they have enough faith, all their troubles and sickness will disappear, and yet *they* are sick or in trouble, or live among those who are sick and troubled. If we accept such a self-centered definition of Christianity and it consistently fails to deliver for us, our conclusion *must* be that we are not a Christian or, at least, an anemic follower of Christ.

It seems doubtful that anyone would refuse a religion which promises the gratification of all needs, wants and desires. How could anyone say "no" to a religion built upon becoming healthy, wealthy and wise just by simply believing? How could anyone resist a religion which promises that you will always be protected from the travesties of nature, the so-called acts of God?

I can't imagine anyone not serving God on the terms that they are to be instantly healed every time they are sick or immediately delivered every time they are in trouble. Even if one wasn't inclined to be religious, it would seem to be the pragmatic thing to adhere to that belief system.

Is Christianity merely a religion meant to be enjoyed? Are we meant to be fulfilled all of the time? Is life truly the self-fulfilling journey being described by some preachers? Any idea that suggests that a person can achieve the Christian life through self-development, self-esteem, and self-assertion is offering a false shortcut that leads only to disappointment and despair.

> **Any suggestion that a person can achieve the Christian life through self- development, self-esteem, and self-assertion leads only to disappointment and despair.**

Of course, a right relationship with God brings a good feeling, but good feelings are not all there is to being a Christian. Jesus elevated religion from the realm of good feeling to that of conviction, sacrifice and responsibility. A. W. Tozer said it best in *Root of the Righteous,* "It appears that too many Christians want to enjoy the thrill of feeling right but are not willing to endure the inconvenience of being right."

I would say if you are looking for a religion that is designed to make you always feel happy, comfortable and untroubled, you should avoid Christianity. A big part of the ministry of Jesus to His disciples was to actually prepare them for His approaching suffering and death. He also makes many references to the fact that those who follow Him will also face persecution and death. He asked them in Mark 10:38-39 if they were willing to "drink the cup that I drink, and be baptized with the baptism that I am baptized with?" When they answered that they were able, He assured them, "You will indeed drink the cup that I drink, and with the baptism I am baptized with you will be baptized" (NKJV). Historical record bears out its fulfillment of this forecast in the suffering, persecution and martyrdom of the disciples.

Hatred and affliction have always followed the witness of the holy life of God's people living in a hostile world. The writer of Hebrews sums up this maltreatment in Hebrews 11:36-38, "Still others had trial of mockings and scourgings, yes, and of chains and imprisonment. They were stoned, they were sawn in two, were tempted, were slain with the sword. They wandered about in sheepskins and goatskins, being destitute, afflicted, tormented -- of whom the world was not worthy. They wandered in deserts and mountains, in dens and caves of the earth" (NKJV).

It is estimated that an army of seventy million has died for the cause of Christ, with over forty-five million (two-thirds) of them having died in the twentieth century. Our generation is witnessing a new century of martyrs. Although it is impossible to verify accurate numbers, some reports indicate that as many as 160,000 Christians have been killed every year since 1990.

So much of what we have heard about God has been nothing but man's attempt to soothe the religious consciousness. In spite of all the human versions, God is not a giant mainframe computer who simply has all information and answers stored away, waiting for the touch of a human hand to access it. He is not merely the Great Mind of the design and creation of this expansive universe, and then He just disappeared. God is indeed the Sovereign Lord of this universe, and yet He stoops to the humble and the contrite of heart.

God is indeed the Sovereign Lord of this universe, and yet He stoops to the humble and the contrite of heart.

There is a demand today for a gospel of the quick-fix. Some turn to Christianity to get "high on Jesus." Others have developed a Quick-Mart mentality toward religion and church. They turn to religion and the church only when their spirits are low and they need a fill-up, or when they need to flush out the rust and dregs of guilt and replace them with fresh hope. Also, some turn to the church when they wish to meet like-minded persons or to find business contacts. This kind of gospel plays especially well to a culture looking for a *McChurch* which can provide them with quick maturity, drive-through service and rapid miracles.

That we are living in a period of religious unrest seems to be an accepted fact. Yet, in the midst of the unrest, there is also a cry for real faith. Unfortunately, instead of the church responding to this cry, some cold, formal, institutionalized churches have sent parishioners scurrying for alternatives, and there is no shortage of alternatives. In earshot of the cry for genuine faith, numerous churches have resorted to a glib faith or to forms of entertainment to attract people to Christianity. It is true that pop religion and entertainment bring lots of people to church. But so do funerals.

The manufacturing of religion for the irreligious has become big business. There is a growing abundance of those who offer facsimiles of Christianity that can do a "more-up-to-date job" of providing what people are looking for in religion. It is, however, a religion which portrays Christianity without God. It is more political and philosophical than theological. The gurus of these contrived religions are attempting to make themselves appear to be great mysteries. They aren't. The Bible characterizes them in Matthew 7:11 as false prophets who will "rise up and deceive many."

Unnatural, frantic work is being done in the Name of God as a cover-up for the lack of personal devotion to God and passion for people. Too many believers are so tired from learning how to serve God that they never get around to actually serving Him. They have attended seminars abundantly. They have been preoccupied for so long with the busyness of the church that they are exasperated.

Matters of faith, dogma, and conviction have often been laid aside while we address the more urgent matters facing the Body of Christ, such as growth, buildings, finances, efficiency and success. It is a classic example of the tyranny of the urgent when pressing or urgent matters take precedence over what is truly important.

From my observation over the past several years of church leadership, many pastors are suffering from fatigue and are close to genuine burnout. It is crucial that ministers be freed from this carousel of habitual performance if we are ever going to see clearly what God is up to on this planet and how the people of God are to be involved. I genuinely believe God desires to give the church a season of equilibrium so that we may truly discover the joys of the Christian life and service!

We do no one a favor by deceiving them to believe that Christianity is reduced to a 'religion' which always provides a ready supply of "just whatever you need at the moment." This is a pathetic substitute for what Christianity truly offers: A personal relationship with the Sovereign God through faith in Jesus Christ, and an eternity with God when this life has ended. Someone has aptly said, *'You can have tons of religion without having an ounce of salvation.'*

Chapter 2

The Encroachment of Pragmatism

It is astounding how many people *use* their religion to authenticate almost every occurrence in life. Perhaps you heard the story of a lady who said she knew it was God's will for her to purchase a dozen doughnuts even though she was on a strict diet. She reasoned, *"Why else would God allow a parking space to open up right in front of the bakery at the exact time the red neon 'Hot Doughnuts Available' sign went on in the window?"* She conveniently forgot to mention that she had circled the block six times before the space became available.

Religion and pragmatism are not strangers. They have paraded together under all sorts of banners. It is the pragmatic side of religion which asks:

- *"How does it work?"*
- *"How much does it cost?"*
- *"What's in it for me?"*
- *"Is it really worth the effort?"*

Pragmatism has become the key word for many Christians today. It's a great time-saver. Pragmatic religion advocates a bottom-line mentality, which permits people to avoid the sacrificial aspects of the gospel and to get straight to the asset column. Pragmatism allows us to be god because we set the rules, establish the objectives and determine the consequences. The pragmatist calls it truth if it works. However, because a belief is useful, it does not make it true.

Pragmatism ties religion to a system of consumerism which advertises:

- Get it!
- Use it!
- Enjoy it!

Pragmatism focuses on a practical set of beliefs which attempt to justify or explain circumstances and to give a formula by which benefits may be obtained. It is this utilitarian aspect of religion which many seem to be advocating. Function becomes more important than belief. Practicality becomes more essential than truth. Validity becomes more legitimate than hope. Efficiency becomes more fundamental than principle. How good it works seems to be that which gives the most convincing evidence nowadays to the value of religion.

This kind of religion fits well into the modern concept of consumerism. Consumerism leaves room for and sometimes encourages buyer's remorse. What happens when you *get it* and it doesn't live up to its publicity? When you try to *use it*, and it doesn't work as advertised? How do you handle it when hurtful circumstances drain away the joy? How do you deal with conflicting emotions?

We probably all know someone who has been disheartened by some aspect of their Christian experience. They know what they have heard and often been told, but what they have experienced is an altogether different thing. If truth is known, there are countless numbers of people who are still fighting personal battles with an inner voice whose name is "Uncertainty". Quite often these battles are fought alone and perhaps with a sense that no one else has ever faced such uncertainties. Recently, I heard of someone who was being encouraged to attend the 'exciting, joyful worship services' at a particular church. But his response to the invitation was disturbing, *"It's difficult to rejoice together when I've spent so much time crying alone."*

Far too many are crying alone, struggling to overcome fears and doubts, and trying to find that level of faith and confident living which sustains them.

Far too many are crying alone, struggling to overcome fears and doubts, and trying to find that level of faith and confident living which sustains them even when circumstances indicate that something has gone terribly wrong. So many of these individuals feel they find no sympathetic understanding when they go to church. What they hear and experience on Sunday doesn't seem to relate with what they are experiencing the rest of the week. Worship should never have as its objective simply to pick up the spirits of distraught people, setting them back on their feet and making them feel better for two or three days. If it doesn't go deeper than that, they will eventually fold up and crumble in despair when their faith is challenged in such a way that no shallow answers seem to make any sense to them.

In today's pragmatic church, oftentimes, a person's grief, tears, suffering and lament are forced underground. There is no place for such pessimistic things. These very real emotions that represent very real events are simply not good for public relations in a pragmatic church. Come to think of it, the Cross may not be good PR, but it is essential for our Salvation. Stephen L. Carter is correct when he says, "We live in a *secular* culture, devoted to sweet reason" (Stephen L. Carter, *The Culture of Disbelief*, (New York: Harper Collins, 1993) pp. 23-24).

For the first time in their lives, many Christians are facing a crisis of faith. That has always been so, but I doubt that any other generation has met a faith crisis any more severe or dangerous than ours. We have witnessed the tragic, personal failures of those in whom we have placed such a high level of confidence. We are being challenged today to reassess our faith through different lenses and many of them distorted. We are being asked to march to the drumbeat of a pragmatic Christianity which bears little resemblance to the New Testament church.

Perhaps the crucial question for us is, *'Are we willing to do God's will out of love for Him alone or do we only do His will for self-interest or because of what He can do for us?'*

Remember Satan's accusation of Job before the throne of God in Job1:9-11. "Does Job fear God for nothing?" Satan replied. "Have you not put a hedge around him and his household and everything he has? You have blessed the work of his hands, so that his flocks and herds are spread throughout the land. But stretch out Your hand and strike everything he has, and he will surely curse You to Your face" (NIV).

Satan is too cunning to endeavor to pick holes in Job's conduct as Job's friends do later. He knows Job is a good man. He knows that his reputation will always withstand extreme scrutiny. What Satan also knows, however, is that the true character of Job's actions is determined by Job's motive? Does Job serve God just for His blessings and for His protection, or does he serve Him because of love? Does Job serve God because of what he expects to gain by it, either in this world or the world to come, or does he serve Him because of *Who* God is?

Job survived all that Satan could unleash upon him for one reason. His motives for serving God were pure. He did not serve God for what he could get out of it, but because he loved and feared God.

Sooner or later, we all have to deal with this matter of motive. Why are we doing what we are doing, and what would it take for God to get us to do more, or for Satan to get us to do less? What are the *hot buttons* which cause us to persevere? Or, what are the *hot buttons* which cause us to withdraw, to sulk, or to retreat? It is often tempting to remain removed from problems or difficulties for which we have no answers readily available.

We will always be capable of tripping ourselves if we do not constantly examine and fully understand our motives and continually return to the divine impulse which causes us to do what is right, regardless of the cost or consequence.

In 2 Corinthians 11:3-4, Paul warns of the possibility of a departure from the Jesus of Scripture. He says, "But I fear, lest somehow, as the serpent deceived Eve by his craftiness, so your minds may be corrupted from the simplicity that is in Christ. For if he who comes preaches another Jesus whom we have not preached, or if you receive a different spirit which you have not received, or a different gospel which you have not accepted – you may well put up with it!" (NKJV)

The great failure of so many in Christendom today is the attempt to override the simplicity of Jesus Christ and the message of the Cross with the substitutes of man's wisdom. The dreadful consequence is that it opens people to receive "a different spirit, or a different Gospel." Other religions have some good ideas and philosophies, but not one of them is capable of providing a Savior. No one but Jesus Christ has the righteousness which is required for fallen mankind to be reconciled to a Holy God. We don't need a guru; we need a Savior.

Other religions have some good ideas and philosophies, but not one of them is capable of providing a Savior.

In her 1952 novel, *Wise Blood*, Flannery O'Connor writes of Hazel Motes, who founds his own religion entitled "The Church Without Christ," and sets out to find a new Jesus who would support his religion. O'Connor seems to write prophetically about our day when many are promoting a *"new Jesus"*, a Jesus of culture rather than the Jesus of Scripture.

There is a vast gulf between the God of Biblical faith and the god of modern folk religion. The god of folk religion is a god of sentimental love, not a holy love. The god of folk religion is treated as "the man upstairs," not as the sovereign God of the universe. The god of folk religion is esteemed as an indulgent father who looks the other way when his children sin, not as the eternal, just judge. The god of folk religion is the middleman between man and his desire. The god of folk religion has manufactured a new Jesus.

Of Jesus, John the Baptist remarked, "...there stands One among you Whom you do not know" (John 1:26, NKJV). John's words have never been more relevant than today. There has never been an age more cut off from the historical Christ, the Messiah, and the Christ of Scripture than ours. Nor has there been a generation which needs Him more. Pragmatic religion alone, regardless of how piously it may be pursued, will never bring one to the point of confidence and faith-filled living God desires for us. It will never bring us into a personal relationship with Jesus Christ that He desires to have with us. Pragmatic thought will never cause anyone to stand firm in their faith through circumstances that cannot be understood nor to face sorrows of life that are so heart-wrenching that answers are not enough.

Pragmatism and *religion* go hand in hand, but pragmatism and *Christianity* don't easily mix. Why? Because:

- Christianity is a covenant community, not a consumer religion.
- Christianity *has* a creed, but it is *not* a creed.
- Christianity follows a set of beliefs, but it is more than

religion.

- Christianity finds its greatest fulfillment in worshipping God, not in personal gratification.
- Christianity finds its absolutes in God, not in appealing circumstances.
- Christianity realizes wholeness through relationships, not through successes and possessions.
- Christianity is not meant to be a part of life or apart from life. It *is* life.

Pragmatism holds to the idea that the only test of probable truth lies in what works best. It places high value on the practical value, outcome or consequence of a thing. The value of the Christian faith can never be reduced to things or consequence. We must never allow our search for cultural relevance of the Gospel to lead us down the path that makes no difference between the culture and the Gospel.

Paul writes, "Even if we or an angel from heaven should preach a gospel other than the one we preached to you, let him be eternally condemned! If anybody is preaching to you a gospel other than what you accepted, let him be eternally condemned!" (Galatians 1:9, NIV)

Chapter 3

The Emptiness of Symbols, Clichés and Traditions

Human life seems to be incurably dependent on traditions and symbols, and so often endeavors to reduce everything, including eternal Truth, down to an effortless cliché. We tend to want to pull it down, remake it in our own image, explain it in our own dialect and wrap it up in the popular style of our culture. God's Truth does not allow itself to be refashioned by popular opinion nor personal need. Therefore, we live in a culture, even in church, that brings confusion and difficulty in grasping the transcendent Truth of the Gospel of our Lord!

Of course, we realize there are good traditions and good symbols, and they have their place in religion. However, the traditions and symbols we have attached to Christianity are wrong if they lead us away from a soul-searching intimacy with Jesus Christ. It seems that intimacy with Jesus is the furthest thing from much preaching and teaching today. Christianity for many seems to be just another technique to be employed in getting to the bottom line. Some have attained the bottom line, and it wasn't what they expected.

Today's generation of church-goers are constantly facing the dangers from mythological traps which Satan is setting all around us. We are being tempted on every side to get rid of the unpleasant aspects of the Christian faith and to settle for shortcuts promised by an increasing number of vendors. There are no shortcuts. God will not be rushed.

People have seen far too many phonies not to be suspicious of anything which hints of pretense. Any suggestion of the artificial conjures up all sorts of mistrust. People are screaming for reality. We have seen far too many cover-ups, learned of far too many codes of silence, and, in general, seen truth sacrificed on the altars of expediency. Appropriateness and political correctness have replaced truthfulness. In a day fraught with misrepresentation, the church needs an open and aggressive attitude toward truth. And yet, some churches seem to have lost sight of the value of truth. Religious practices and traditions tend to build a rigid crust around the human heart, prohibiting it from feeling anything which does not live up to the expectations of stated dogma and shielding it from accepting fresh impulses from the Spirit. Our heart must always be open to God.

So many practices in today's church do not rise out of an inquisition for truth but result from the recoil of barren Christianity. A church which is not fulfilling the Great Commission or executing those things which, according to the Word, are primary to the church's being, is often pressed into surreal activities. Most of these surreal events look and sound good but are of no earthly value to the kingdom of God.

Many regular church attendees would probably be amazed to know how unintelligible much of our religious jargon is to the non-church attendees. Unchurched people are being increasingly repelled by religious clichés. Those outworn and overused truisms are so out of touch with where most people truly live. It is time for us to present the Word of God rather than the puny words we sometimes use to explain God and why He does what He does. It is most often the glib clichés about God and the Christian faith which create the most mistrust in the hearts of believers and also before a watching world.

Some Christians seem to have a terrific propensity for using such language at the most inopportune times. Several years ago, I witnessed one such time of inappropriate and confusing language. I, along with another minister, had been asked to participate in the funeral of a one-year-old child. The parents were, of course, terribly distraught and were struggling to cope with why God would allow their child to die at such a young age. The minister who preceded me in the ceremony seemed to have all the answers to the many questions of this child's untimely death all figured out. Unfortunately, his answers were not merely unhelpful for the parents but were hurtful and confusing for this grieving family. Frankly, his comments regarding the reason as to why God took their child made me quite angry.

Early in his remarks, he called attention to the beautiful floral arrangement which draped the little casket. He said, "You will notice how the florist has taken flowers of all sizes and descriptions to make such a beautiful arrangement. That's why God has taken this little one from our midst. He needed a little rose bud to make His garden complete."

I sensed a slow burn emerging in my spirit as I felt the urge to stand up and shout, *"That is not true! The God we serve would not do such an obscene thing."* I didn't stand up at that moment, but I did try to set the record straight when my turn came to speak. I said to this group of family and friends, *"I don't know why God allowed this to happen, but I can assure you that He didn't do it for His own entertainment. I do know that He loves you, and that He is here to comfort you, and someday you will fully understand the answers to all your questions."*

Many of those perceptions are based more on temporal culture rather than God's divine revelation of Himself.

We each have attached some meaning to God. We have some definite ideas, images and a mental picture of the God we think about, pray to and worship. Many of those perceptions are based more on temporal culture rather than God's divine revelation of Himself. Wrong concepts of God may inflict antagonisms which take years to overcome, and, sadly, some are never resolved. It's no wonder that some people have such hazy and indefinite ideas about God and Christianity. They have too often been confronted with ideas about God and Christianity that do not correspond with the authenticity of Scripture and treat with contempt any personal queries.

I recently spoke to a student who shared a story about a friend of his who was, in his words, "very intelligent and had great potential to do something for God." His friend had been devastated by a "prophetic word" that proved to be false. His concern was whether or not his friend would ever be the same. Probably not. But what would be helpful is for this young man to see a demonstration of the genuine prophetic Spirit of God. He needs to learn from a seasoned, wise mentor how to listen and respond to future such "prophetic" utterances.

When we don't know the *why* it would be better for us just to come clean and say so. It is surely more pleasing to God than for us to fake an answer. I'm positive it is more helpful for us to just be honest with people when they are struggling to get a handle on true faith. It's actually okay for the Christian to sometimes admit, *'I really don't know why, but I know God, and I trust Him to make sense out of all that happens.'*

I can't begin to tell you how many suffering people I have seen devastated by apparently well-meaning Christians who, like Job's comforters, reflect on the character of the sufferer by implying, *'If you were all that you should be, this wouldn't be happening to you.'* Often, when life hurts and catastrophes are overwhelming, our responses are not only unscriptural but often undermine the very faith in an individual's life we need to strengthen!

The Scripture records a discussion between Jesus and His disciples about this very issue in John 9:1-3. "Now as Jesus passed by, He saw a man who was blind from birth. And His disciples asked Him, saying, 'Rabbi, who sinned, this man or his parents, that he was born blind?' Jesus answered, 'Neither, this man nor his parents sinned, but that the works of God should be revealed in him" (NKJV).

Of course, sin has consequences in all our lives. If we fill our lives with terrible choices and unhealthy habits, we will reap the consequence of disease, broken relationships and various outcomes of sadness. But, Christ is not limited in His healing, in His salvation to redeem, or in His power to restore and change the course of our lives regardless of our past.

God is not far away or unreachable. He is not off in some far away corner of the universe waiting to be aroused by our religious incantations. He is near. He is a Person and can be met as a Person. Hear Him as He declares: "Am I a God near at hand,' says the LORD, 'And not a God afar off? Can anyone hide himself in secret places, so I shall not see him?' says the LORD; 'Do I not fill heaven and earth?' says the Lord" (Jeremiah 23:23, 24, NKJV).

Some time ago while going through my files, I came across some prose I had written several years ago. I share this with you not because I consider it good prose, but because I think it reflects how I have often felt about some of my circumstances. Perhaps you can also relate.

> *God,*
> *Why don't You come down*
> *and show this world that You're still around?*
> *You've been mocked,*

scorned and denied.
Some have even said You were dead.
It wouldn't take much;
just part a sea,
set fire to a bush,
write with Your finger on a table of stone,
or open up the ground and swallow up
those who deny You.
You've done it all before,
why not do it again?
Just come down,
and show the world You are still around.
Whenever I pray this, God responds:
"I did come down, in the form of human flesh,
and look what selfish, religious people did to me."

Christianity is not some superstitious concoction which can only be accessed by runaway emotions. It is based on revelation and historical facts and must be approached with both head and heart. The Christian faith goes beyond reason, but it is not nonsense. It is foolish to those who are blinded and hardened in their heart by Satan.

Paul writes in I Corinthians 1:18-21, "For the word of the cross is folly (foolishness) to those who are perishing, but to us who are being saved it is the power of God. For it is written: 'I will destroy the wisdom of the wise, and the discernment of the discerning I will thwart.' Where is the one who was wise? Where is the scribe? Where is the debater of this age? Has not God made foolish the wisdom of the world? For since, in the wisdom of God, the world did not know God through wisdom, it pleased God through the folly (foolishness) of what we preach to save those who believe" (ESV).

We can fully trust in the unshakeable Truth of the Gospel. We don't have to orchestrate or manipulate the message of this Truth to make it more palpable, relevant or acceptable.

Part 2

Integrity and the Heart of the Matter

S ome people seem to feel that it is their everlasting obligation
to defend God's reputation. They appear to operate by some
unwritten code which says "don't embarrass God by telling the
truth."

There are two basic problems with any attempt to protect God's
reputation. First, God's reputation can never be impaired by any
sincere inquiry. In fact, He invites inquiry. Since Christianity is
about the One who is called Truth, honest examination can never
be out of order. Unaddressed questions and ignored doubt will
eventually take you down. Second, what we are protecting is not
always God's reputation but our own.

Most of us are reluctant to admit we have identified with
'doubting Thomas'. Thomas said he would not be satisfied until
he saw the scars in the hands of Christ and the wound in His
side. In John 20:19-24, Christ appeared to His disciples after His
resurrection, and all the disciples were there with the exception of
Thomas. Christ first showed His disciples, with the exception of

Thomas, these scars so their doubts would be alleviated and their faith increased.

When the disciples recounted this great visitation of Christ, Thomas said in John 20:25, "Unless I see in His hands the print of the nails, and put my finger into the print of the nails, and put my hand into His side, I will not believe." Verses 26-28 continue, "And after eight days His disciples were again inside, and Thomas with them. Jesus came, the doors being shut, and stood in the midst and said, 'Peace to you!' Then He said to Thomas, 'Reach your finger here, and look at My hands; and reach your hand here, and put it into My side. Do not be unbelieving, but believing.' And Thomas answered and said to Him, 'My Lord and My God!'" (NKJV)

We all understand that Thomas had to see for himself, but the reality is that Christ chose to reveal Himself to Thomas. He loved Thomas, and Christ allowed the questions and doubts Thomas had to be answered. Thomas was later martyred in India for the Truth of the Gospel. Christ preferred that Thomas believe his brothers' account of His appearing to them, and declared that those who have never seen and still believe would be blessed. But, Christ *did* come to respond to the doubts of Thomas.

Unfortunately, we have not always been encouraged to put our questions to the test against the truth of the Gospel. For too long, we have been motivated to reject or disguise our true feelings in preference to putting the *best possible face on our circumstances* so as not to send negative messages to unbelievers.

It's very unlikely than many of us have ever considered confessing our struggles to an unbeliever. I have a feeling that would undoubtedly catch an unbeliever off guard. We need to be assured that the embracing of truth – any truth – does not place us in conflict with our faith in God or His Word. Christian vitality is never hindered by being honest. A search for truth is embodied as foundational in the Christian faith. From what I perceive, this postmodern age is much more open to receive a testimony reflecting the authenticity of life than it is some fabrication. The world is not turned off by the Christian faith. It is turned off by simulated Christianity.

The world is not turned off by the Christian faith. It is turned off by simulated Christianity.

Let's face it, all of us have struggled with troublesome questions regarding the Christian life, the church, fellow believers and, yes, even troubling questions about God. Though none of us has escaped the distressing anguish of these probing questions, we probably were shamed if we ever did get the courage to raise them, and were most likely encouraged to push aside any such inquiries. The problem is that an accumulation of unaddressed questions has a tendency to gang up on you, to catch you at some weak moment and take you down in despair.

Almost casually I asked a friend and personal mentor of many years, *"How are you?"*

"Not so good," he replied.

"What's happened?" I inquired.

"Oh, nothing out of the ordinary. It's just the accumulation of things which have happened over the past several years which have

finally gotten through to me."

Although shocking at the moment and because I least expected it from this particular man, I concluded that his situation is probably not uncommon. In fact, after checking up on my own feelings, I came to the conclusion that I probably wasn't too far behind him.

The truth is that a person's deep faith is not usually affected by a single catastrophic event. It's more like a grinding deterioration. The constant dripping of water will eventually wear away steel. We often deal with the proverbial 'frog in the kettle' syndrome. The story is often told that if you place a frog in boiling water, it will immediately jump out. But, if you place a frog in cool water and begin to gradually turn the heat up, the frog will not notice the change and eventually be boiled alive. Like any fable, this story serves its purpose whether or not it's based upon something literally true. It illustrates the gradual accumulation of dangerous catastrophes that eventually erode or destroy a person's faith.

The person who wants to be honest in his or her pursuit of Christianity can never be passive toward truth. Truth must be sought openly and aggressively, and once found, embraced and shared. The enviable people are those who decide to face the facts squarely, to understand themselves, and to know the real meaning of the Christian life. Walter Brueggeman says, "There is no doubt that ministry is robbed of vitality and authority by participating in a charade of protecting self and others from the truth of the gospel" (Walter Brueggeman, *Hopeful Imagination*, (Philadelphia: Fortress Press, 1986) p. 28).

Our misunderstandings about the Gospel of Jesus Christ often

come early in our walk with Him. Thomas Merton inquires: "How
many people are there in the world today who have 'lost their faith'
along with the vain hopes and illusions of their childhood. What
they called 'faith' was just one among all the other illusions. They
placed all their hope in a certain sense of spiritual peace, of comfort,
of interior equilibrium, of self-respect. Then when they began to
struggle with the real difficulties and burdens of mature life, when
they became aware of their own weakness, they lost their peace,
they lost their precious self-respect, and it became impossible for
them to 'believe.' That is to say it became impossible for them to
comfort themselves, to reassure themselves, with the images and
concepts they found reassuring in childhood" (Thomas Merton,
New Seeds of Contemplation, (New York: The Abby of Gethsemane,
Inc. 1961) p. 187).

Some time ago, I was reflecting on some impressions of Christianity as formed early in my own journey of faith. I remembered
what may have been the first time I realized my religious formula
did not work for me. Not surprisingly, it is often those early
imprints which are the most deeply ingrained and, consequently,
those into which one least likes to inquire.

I must have been every bit of eleven years old. An evangelist
I once heard preached from 2 Kings 5 about the prophet Elijah
commanding Naaman to go to the Jordan River and dip himself
seven times in the muddy water. Of course, the purpose was for
Naaman to obey the word of the Lord through Elijah so that Naaman's leprosy would be healed. It struck a personal chord with me.
No, I didn't have leprosy. But I did have something from which I

wanted to be cleansed just as Naaman had been.

For most of my life, I had worn long-sleeve shirts to hide a large and very obvious birth mark on my left arm. It was the cause of a great many verbal slurs, especially when I forgot and wore a short sleeve shirt to school.

"Hey, Vest. When are you going to wash that rust off your arm?" A few times the verbal offense provoked a physical retaliation on my part.

Hearing the evangelist tell the story of Naaman was the answer I was looking for. If God did it for Naaman, He would surely do it for me. I knew I couldn't get to the Jordan River, but I figured Double Branch would work just as well. I didn't tell anyone. I jumped on my bicycle after I got home from school the next day and scurried down to Double Branch about a mile behind my home.

You probably guessed it. I dipped my arm seven times in Double Branch. I really believed my arm would come up clear of the birth mark upon the seventh dip. I had already planned which short-sleeve shirt I would wear to school the next day, and how I would tell all my friends that God healed me. My motives were pure. At least, I believed they were.

I stood there on the bank of Double Branch, waiting. Nothing happened. It took me a long time to get over the disappointment. Why didn't God heal me? I didn't know why God had not removed that birth mark. I just knew it didn't work for me as it had for Naaman.

I was too embarrassed to tell anyone about it, or to seek biblical counsel. Unfortunately, Satan actually used that incident for a long time as an intimidation to my prayers. *"Remember Double Branch,"* he would whisper whenever I asked God for anything. *"God's not listening to you,"* he would chide. The Double Branch incident faded into insignificance compared with later showdowns with the reality that God does not always work as I think He should.

A more recent incident caused even more questions regarding my understanding of healing and how God chooses to allocate it. For at least three days and nights, I lay in the hospital with a fever which at times escalated to the point of requiring that I had to be covered with crushed ice and alcohol. With each approaching evening, the doctors told my wife to prepare for the worst since I might not live through the night. I had contracted typhoid fever while in the service of my church's missions department. From what the attending physicians said, I came about as close to death as an individual can without actually dying.

After I was discharged from the hospital, and while I was still in the process of the long recovery, I decided to return to my office. I met a preacher friend of mine who remarked, *"Hey doc, I hear you've been sick."*

"Yes, I have," I replied.

"What was the problem?" he asked.

I told him the story of my fever and the fact that I almost died.

"Where in the world did you come into contact with typhoid fever and what were your symptoms?" he asked.

I told him the whole story, and he responded thoughtfully, *"You know, I was in that very same hotel in that same little village several years ago. And, I'm sure I contracted the same disease."* *"At least,"* he said, *"I had the symptoms you've just described."*

What did you do?" I asked.

The man's response surprisingly took me off guard. *"Well, I just got down to business with God, and told Him that I was there doing business for Him and He had to help me. And He did. You know, I preached that same night, and many people came to know the Lord."*

I replied, *"That's good."*

But it wasn't good. At least, what it did to me at the moment wasn't good. I went straight home, fell across my bed and began to cry, which was totally out of the ordinary for me. My wife came into the room to ask what was wrong. *"I don't understand it,"* I exclaimed. *"Why did God heal* (I called the brother's name) *and yet let me almost die?"*

How often have hurting Christians been even more tragically devastated by withering remarks of some unthinking person who implies in various ways, *'when you have enough faith in God as I do, maybe He will heal you.'* Words mouthed without thought or without coming from the heart are at best insensitive. At worst, they can even be destructive.

Hiding behind the masks of self-righteousness, self-made perfection, and false beliefs can be fatal. We need to come to a point where we can confess, *"God, I realize that I am weak. My questions are many. Help me to experience your Presence so I may rejoice in your glory."* Only when we have acknowledged our weaknesses, are we ready to move forward to a deeper relationship with God.

We are all immigrants from the past. Unfortunately, some of us get stuck there. There is no sin in having one's mind vexed by questions or doubts. The sin is to sit quietly, nursing the doubt without facing it. We must make the great adventure and correct our conception as new truth is made clear to us.

Do I understand everything that God permits to happen? Of course, I don't. Do I trust Him always to know what is best in light of my eternal destiny? Yes, and that trust in Him is all He asks of us.

Chapter 4

Losing Religion and Finding Faith

When tragedy strikes, do we cry, '*Oh, God, why has this happened to me?*' When difficulties come in like a tsunami, do we feel as though we are losing our faith?

If we answer yes to either of these questions, it may be that our trust has not truly been in God but in our own well-being. Oftentimes, we trust more in what God can do for us than we actually trust in God Himself. When we feel we have lost God's help, we feel as though we are losing our faith. As Job reveals to us in Scripture, if our faith is truly in God, we could lose faith in everything else and still have faith in God.

Is it possible that the faith we have defined for ourselves is a faith in our own well-being rather than faith in a sovereign God? How much trouble and sickness would it take to cause us to abandon faith altogether? How much difficulty would it take for us to look elsewhere for solutions?

Howard Kushner warns, "The misfortunes of good people are not only a problem to the people who suffer and to their families. They are a problem to everyone who wants to believe in a just and fair and livable world. They inevitably raise questions about the goodness, the kindness, even the existence of God" (Howard Kushner, *When Bad Things Happen To Good People* (New York: Avon Books, 1981) p. 67).

Through the crucibles of living and through a lifetime of searching Scripture, I am convinced that many Christians have adopted a definition of faith which is far too narrow. Faith is not something you can pick up when you need it and lay it down when you don't. Faith doesn't rise or fall depending on circumstances.

I recently heard of an agnostic businessman who was asked, *"How did you lose your faith?"*

"Lose my faith?" he responded. *"I didn't lose it. I just put it away in a drawer and decided I would pull it out when I needed it. But when I went back for it, it wasn't there."*

Faith is something you have to live with in the darkness and in the light of day. It is faith that keeps you believing in the grace, mercy and sovereignty of God, even in the midst of depressing circumstances. Brennan Manning says, "In faith there is a movement and development. Each day something is new. To be a Christian, faith has to be alive and growing. It cannot be static, finished, settled. When Scripture, prayer, worship, ministry become routine, they are dead" (Brennan Manning, *The Ragamuffin Gospel* (Multnomah Publishers, Inc., Sisters, Oregon, 2002) p. 61).

Faith is certainly not a leap in the dark, but if you wait until you get everything figured out, you will never move. Faith divorced from knowledge is mere superstition, but it is more than a mere assent to facts. In Biblical terms, faith is belief. It is being convinced that certain things are true. Faith is trusting in God that He is always in charge and He will always prevail, regardless of circumstances. Faith is acting on what you believe. It is confidence, trust, and submission to the authority of God in our lives.

> ## Faith is certainly not a leap in the dark, but if you wait until you get everything figured out, you will never move.

Unanswered prayers have probably created as much cynicism regarding Christianity as has anything. And, if we are totally honest, prayer is perhaps the most confusing and mysterious aspect of the Christian faith.

Huck Finn put it in these words:

> *"Miss Watson...she took me into the closet and prayed... but nothing come of it. She told me to pray every day...and whatever I asked for I would get it. But it warn't so...I tried it. Once I got a fish-line...but no hooks. It warn't any good to me without hooks. I tried for the hooks three or four times...but somehow I couldn't make it work.*
>
> *"By and by, one day, I asked Miss Watson to try for me... but she said I was foolish. She never told me why...and I couldn't make it out no way. I just sat down one time in the woods and had a long think about it. I says to myself:*

'If a body can get anything they pray for...why don't Deacon
Winn get back the money he lost on pork? Why can't the
widow get back her silver snuff-box that was stole? Why
can't Miss Watson fat up?'

Mark Twain, who in actuality put the words in Huck Finn's mouth, apparently believed that way about prayer all of his life. From all we know, Mark Twain died believing that way.

I don't yet understand why God chooses to answer some prayers and not others. I have prayed for some sick people who were miraculously healed. I have prayed for others who died. I honestly can't say that my faith was any stronger in the first case than the latter. And, from what I remember, I could tell no difference in the faith of persons for whom I prayed. I do, however, believe that God does make the choice. If He is the sovereign God we say He is, then the answer to prayer is not what we want but what He wills. There is an immeasurable difference between saying that God can answer prayer and saying that God will answer prayer in the way we wish. God is sovereign, and He is faithful!

Sometimes we tritely answer this conundrum by suggesting that God *always* answers prayer with a *yes, no,* or *wait.* While this explanation has the advantage of never being wrong, it also fails to explain why we see results to some of our prayers and not others. If God says *yes,* it may happen immediately, tomorrow or sometime in the future. If God says *no,* then we know He has answered, but we are not going to get that for which we have asked. If God says *wait,* the question then becomes *'How long?'* or *'Could I have to wait forever?'*

We are encouraged in John 14:13-14, "And whatever you ask in My name, that I will do, that the Father may be glorified in the Son. If you ask anything in My name, I will do it" (NKJV). Surely, we are aware that not every one of our prayers will be answered in the manner in which we think they should be answered. So, what does Jesus really mean here?

First, we pray in Jesus' Name. This means that we come to the throne of God through the grace and blood of Jesus Christ, without which we have no access to God. We come before Him with confidence, because we are reconciled to the Father through Jesus Christ. Also, when we pray in Jesus' Name, this means our prayer should be in accordance with the will of Jesus. God will give us anything that is in keeping with the will of His Son.

We come before Him with confidence, because we are reconciled to the Father through Jesus Christ.

It is a tremendous sign of maturity when the believer can peacefully face his or her difficulties by following the admonition of James 4:15, "... you ought to say, 'If the Lord wills, we shall live and do this or that'" (NKJV). The calm, faithful, patient, godly life has much impact on the lives of those who watch from a distance. You can be certain, they are watching and listening. That's why James tells us that we "take the prophets, who spoke in the name of the Lord, as an example of suffering and patience" (James 5:10, NKJV).

There is nothing like a rendezvous with what Thomas Merton calls, "mature reality" to cause you to probe deeply into your system of faith. I have lived long enough and have faced many "mature realities" that cause one to ask *"Why, God?"* I've known scores of people who indicated that everything was all right, but I knew in my heart everything was not all right. In reality, so did they. They just wouldn't talk about it. For years, I've observed people who pace merrily along with no questions asked, feeling that it was wrong to ask *why*. I've also watched far too many of those same people crash and burn in their Christian experience.

My rendezvous with a crushing reality came in a Chattanooga, Tennessee doctor's office when my late wife, Iris, and I were informed that she had pancreatic cancer. I was manifestly more shaken by the news than she was. After we were alone, Iris assured me that there was nothing to fear because God was in control. That was all I needed. I knew that if God was in control, everything was going to be alright. Later I would struggle with that assurance and with the debate that has lingered for centuries among Christians: *'Is there a difference between God being in control and the sovereignty of God?'*

As Iris lingered in a coma following surgery, the mere thought that I was struggling with the question *'How much is God really in control?'* truly terrified me. I had never grappled with the big ideas of creation or eternity, but now was facing the question we all have to face sooner or later: *'If God is in control, why is this happening to me?'* Trouble, sorrow and suffering always seem to propel us toward serious thoughts about God as creator and controller.

The sovereignty of God is the biblical teaching that all things are under God's rule and that nothing happens without His direction or permission. God works *all* things, not just *some* things, but *all* things according to the counsel of His own will. Paul addresses this issue in Ephesians 1:11, "In Him also we have obtained an inheritance, being predestined according to the purpose of Him who works all things according to the counsel of His will" (NKJV). His purposes are all-inclusive and never thwarted, and absolutely nothing takes Him by surprise. The prophet writes in Isaiah 46:11 "… The man who executes My counsel, from a far country. Indeed I have spoken *it*; I will also bring it to pass. I have purposed *it*; I will also do it" (NKJV).

God is the Almighty, Omnipotent God. He is the Creator and Sustainer of all that exists. There is none higher, none more worthy of worship and honor. He can be counted on for our salvation, and He can be counted on to safely carry us through times of difficulty so that nothing touches us that is not in keeping with His desires for us. He can be counted on to keep all the promises He has made to us.

He is not aloof nor is He distant like the deistic understanding of a God who created the universe but then left it to run according to natural laws with little or no intervention on His part. This is where the tension comes.

Perhaps you, like the Psalmist in Psalm 88, asked God in your time of greatest need, why He has deserted you. Perhaps, like me, there have been those times when you've worn holes in the knees of your trousers from praying and, yet nothing seems to change. The God you worship seems absent when you need Him the most. Old Testament characters like Job and Jeremiah wondered aloud about where God was and if He had plugged His ears and was not listening.

I know that God does care about our present circumstances. That is why Jesus came in human flesh and walked among us. God not only didn't have His ears plugged, He actually took on our form – human ears. He heard firsthand the groans of the world. He heard the cries of the sick and the needy. He still hears all the cries of those in pain!

But we must never forget that we live in a fallen world. We suffer because we live in a fallen world system. When sin entered the world, death also entered, as well as chronic pain, illness, disease, insult, broken promises, ungodly intentions of evil men and all that you and I endure in our personal sorrow. God is aware and is never aloof when one person suffers at the hand of someone else. He sees when a drunk driver kills an innocent child or when a Holocaust is raging against His own people.

We must take our questions and doubts to God rather than allowing them to become a wedge in our relationship with Him.

We must take our questions and our doubts to God rather than allowing them to become a wedge in our relationship with Him. If we follow the example of the Psalmist, we cry out to God as though taking Him to task for our problems. Job, who had endured unspeakable suffering said, "My ears had heard of You but now my eyes have seen You" (Job 42:5, NIV).

Our lives are a series of events, and until we've reached the conclusion of these events, it's difficult to know exactly why things are happening as they do. In the Old Testament teachings of Jacob, we see how God was teaching an entire generation of God's people about how He wanted them to live through the series of events that would take place in their lives and in their nation. The focus and the story's key character is Jacob's son, Joseph. This story about Joseph begins in Genesis 37 and ends in Genesis 50, and exemplifies the inability to understand a series of events until God reveals it.

Joseph was kidnapped by his own brothers who, in a jealous rage, threw him in a pit. Joseph was taken to Egypt by the men who rescued him from the pit, but they later sold him into slavery. He was bought by an honest man named Potipher, who entrusted great responsibilities of his household to Joseph. Things seemed to be turning around for Joseph, but the series of difficult events continued when Potipher's wife falsely accused Joseph of such a horrific deed that he is thrown into prison. While in prison, he meets two men who had once been royal servants for the Pharaoh of Egypt. One man had been a cupbearer and the other a baker in the household of Pharaoh. While in prison, these two men had troubling dreams and Joseph interprets each man's dream. The interpretation of the cupbearer's dream gave great hope of release, but the baker's dream was about his eventual death in the prison. Joseph asked the cupbearer to remember him when he is set free and restored in the Pharaoh's service.

Joseph was hopeful that he too could finally be released from prison for the good he had done for the cupbearer. Joseph waited, but when the cupbearer was released and once again a servant to the Pharaoh, he forgot about Joseph for several years.

Genesis 41 records a time when the Pharaoh has a tormenting dream and asks for someone among his advisors to interpret his troubling dream. None of Pharaoh's counselors were able to give meaning to Pharaoh's dream. At that point, the cupbearer is reminded of 'his shortcomings' and tells the Pharaoh he knows someone in prison who can interpret his dream. When Joseph is brought before Pharaoh, he interprets the dream, is released from prison, and is given a place of leadership and honor, second only to Pharaoh.

The years that Joseph faithfully served in the house of Pharaoh were, obviously, better than a pit, slavery, false accusations, and prison. No one can know for sure, but Joseph must have questioned why he was still separated from his father, his family, and friends in Canaan.

Years passed and Joseph's brothers were sent by their father, Jacob, to find grain in Egypt because of a great famine. The brothers are brought before Joseph but do not recognize him. Joseph sets in motion a plan to have his brothers bring their father from Canaan to Egypt. This well-known story ends with the joyful reunion of Joseph with his father, and the forgiveness and restoration of his brothers who had begun this series of sorrowful and painful events.

At most any point during the seemingly devastating series of events in Joseph's life, if someone had asked him about the good God he served, what would have been his answer? How would he have described Him? But, as the Prime Minister of Egypt and after he had been reunited with his family, Joseph would have probably described the goodness of God very differently. It was only in retrospect that Joseph could see more clearly that the series of events that had happened to him was for good.

Joseph explained and gave perspective to the series of events that had led him and also his brothers to that day in Genesis 45: 5-8, "Do not be grieved or angry with yourselves, because you sold me here; for God sent me before you to preserve life. For these two years the famine has been in the land, and there are still five years in which there will be neither plowing nor harvesting. God sent me before you to preserve posterity for you in the earth, and to save your lives by a great deliverance. So now it was not you who sent me here, but God; and He has made me a father to Pharaoh, and lord of all his house, and a ruler throughout all the land of Egypt" (NASB).

This is a beautiful understanding of the sovereignty of God explained, but not many of us have the knowledge of what God is accomplishing through our sorrow or circumstances in the moment. God may choose to reveal all the answers to us in the midst of our trial or at the end of our lives, but certainly when we enter His Presence and live with Him eternally, all will be understood.

> ## God may reveal all the answers in the midst of our trial or at the end of our lives, but when we enter His Presence and live with Him eternally, all will be understood.

It is difficult when we realize that we might not understand all the things that happen in our life. We must trust the God Who is worthy of that trust. It is not a blind leap of faith to trust in the God of the Scriptures! Truth is revealed in Scripture and the character of God is revealed in Christ. When we have faith in the character and Truth of God, then we can stand in those situations that make absolutely no sense in the moment.

Christ was assaulted by Satan's temptations and accusations. He understood what it was like to be rejected and betrayed by those closest to Him. He also asked the question that we often ask, "My God, My God, why have you forsaken me?" He walked this earth and in His pain in the final breaths of His life, He asked our questions. He asked my questions.

We saw that God did not abandon His Son in His hour of greatest need. We saw God's answer three days later when God raised Him to life again. Because of this promise of life, we have hope for our future. Despite the turmoil and chaos that life's sorrow can bring and despite what it might seem at any given moment in the series of events in your life, there is one thing that is true. God is with us! He never leaves us, and He never forsakes us. He knows the pain, and He hears our prayers.

In the weeks following Iris' death, I first began to realize how imperfectly I really understood God's sovereignty and prayer. In light of the outlook of her physical condition and the prognosis that her recovery was not at all promising, a call for prayer went out all around the world. I have never been aware of a greater prayer vigil in my life. My family and I, of course, spent all the time we were allowed in the intensive care unit at the hospital with Iris. The rest of the time, we spent trying to either rest or pray. We were blessed by many of our extended family and friends who came into the room during visiting hours to offer prayer, and to let us know that their church was also praying.

Those voices of kindness and sincere encouragement of friends and colleagues during this time were priceless to us! The faithfulness of God was exemplified in their lives. But there were other voices that brought a feeling of hope through some 'predictions' about Iris' recovery. They proved to not be true. Someone actually told us they had received a *confirmation* that Iris was going to not only revive from her coma but also her full recovery was *just around the corner.*

Shortly after her death, as I knelt by my bed to pray, the memory of the incidents of that day overwhelmed me with waves of doubt, sorrow and questions. I found it impossible to pray. My mind was flooded with emotion as I recalled someone advising me, *"Hold on, because her death was a ploy of the devil to try to discourage me."* Another person had said, *"This is a trial from God, because He is preparing you for greater service."*

As unanswerable questions and cruel confusion began to sweep over my mind, 'something' stirred deeply in my spirit, and I rose from my knees. I immediately turned to my left and shouted aloud to the unseen but very real Accuser,

"Devil, if this is you, you may as well give it up! You know that I am not going to abandon my trust in God."

Then, I turned to my right and shouted again, but this time addressing my God Who had never left me nor had forsaken me,

"God, if this is You, and You are putting me to a test, go ahead and give me the final exam. You know, I'm going to pass!"

I didn't have a clearer understanding in that moment, and I

didn't experience a great revelation of answers. My life hurt at a depth where answers were inadequate. But, I did know that God had reminded me that He was trustworthy, and He gave me faith to stand when I could not understand. I did know that His Spirit had "invited" me to stand in His Presence and allowed me to directly address all my doubts, questions and confusion.

Our search for personal integrity must begin with being totally honest with God. One of the beautiful things about the God we serve is that He doesn't mind directness. In fact, He invites it. One Jewish scholar says that wrestling with God is essential to being a Jew, and suggests that if you are too comfortable with God it is probably because you have made Him into your own image (a direct reference to Christians).

The Book of Job became a great source of strength for me during the time of the loss of my late wife. In some ways, we have created our own myths even about Job. There are probably too many sermons about Job's positive dealing with his problems and not enough from a holistic view, so we get a distorted picture. A complete reading of Job reveals that there were times of pain, anguish, disappointment, confusion, and betrayal. Any emotion you can imagine, Job seems to have experienced them all.

Job had, with great wordiness, addressed his questions and discontentment to his friends, but in Job 7:11-19, he turns his disapproval to God, "Therefore I will not restrain my mouth; I will speak in the anguish of my spirit; I will complain in the bitterness of my soul. Am I a sea, or a sea serpent, That You set a guard over me? When I say, 'My bed will comfort me, My couch will ease my complaint.' Then You scare me with dreams and terrify me with visions, So that my soul chooses strangling and death rather than my body. I loathe my life; I would not live forever. Let me alone, For my days are but a breath. "What is man, that You should exalt him, That You should set Your heart on him, That You should visit him every morning, And test him every moment? How long? Will You not look away from me, And let me alone till I swallow my saliva?" (NKJV)

God allows and even invites directness. But, as Job found out, it is definitely a two-way street. God reserves the right to push back. God seems to be saying to Job, *'Okay. Now that you have been direct with me, I have a few things to tell you.'* What He said to Job is recorded in Job 38-41. In these chapters, we see that Job had learned suffering is not punishment. It is not a sign of God's anger. His pain was not the pain of the avenger's whip. The pain was not a result of the consequences of Job's sin. It was the pain of the surgeon's scalpel.

Not getting in touch with our honest feelings can lead to disillusionment. Disillusionment leads to disenchantment. Disenchantment leads to cynicism. Cynicism leads to a plethora of other debilitating emotions and actions, most of which are self-destructive. It is only when we are honest with God that we can be honest with ourselves and others.

As I have learned by both having been the judge and the judged, no one should ever judge unless he or she asks in absolute honesty what they may have done in a similar situation. It was after the death of his wife that C. S. Lewis declared, "Not that I am in much danger of ceasing to believe in God. The real danger is of coming to believe such dreadful things about Him" *(A Grief Observed).*

It was during my struggles with Iris' passing when my real education concerning prayer began. I realized that when I was quiet long enough for God to speak to me, prayer became what I had always imagined it to be: deep, heartfelt, and intimate communication. However, up until this time, I had done all the talking. Now God did the talking, and I did the listening. What I learned during this time has shaped what I now feel to be the essence of spiritual praying. Prayer is communication, but communication is a two-way street. It is connecting with that still small voice that signified God's Presence to Elijah in I Kings 19:11-15.

Prayer is communication, but communication is a two-way street. It is connecting with that still small voice that signifies God's Presence.

Elijah connected with God's Voice as he stood in a cave of uncertainty and fear where he experienced the illusion of helplessness and hopelessness. In Elijah's longing to hear the Voice of God, he could have been fooled in thinking God's Voice must certainly be in the great, strong wind that broke the mountain rocks in pieces where he stood. Or surely God's Voice would be in the earthquake or possibly in the fire. But, after the great fire, earthquake and strong wind, Elijah continued to listen for God's Voice. He did not get caught up in the howling, loud circumstances whirling around him. He waited. God spoke in a still small Voice, and Elijah heard it and stood in God's Presence.

God does hear our prayer, and He is not silent. The problem is that we are not always prepared for God's response. A contemporary song by lyrist John Hiatt says, "You wouldn't know a burning bush if it blew up in your face."

I have learned that not all prayers are answered as we wish. I am also convinced that we err by making people feel "faithless" when their prayers are not apparently answered. Always leave room for the miraculous, but be prepared to trust God when there is no miracle that changes our circumstances.

Prayer is not making demands on God. It is an attempt to put ourselves in harmony with His will. God is a Person, and through prayer we meet Him as a Person. Prayer is much broader than petition. It is praise, it is worship, and it is fellowship. Prayer is an act of yielding. Prayer should not be viewed as an attempt to get God to do what we want Him to do. It is our attempt to put ourselves in such an attitude that God can work through us. Prayer is submission to Him and to His will.

It is time to lose our shallow religion and find true faith. True faith prevails. True faith quickly hurdles the *"Why me?"* question and says, *"Now that it has happened, how do I deal with it?"* True faith is best tested against the crucibles of everyday living, against disappointments and confusion.

Essential to our own personal holiness is the genuine desire to be "tested of the Lord." In a world where every obstacle was removed and in which someone could not keep oneself from doing right, there would be no *real* morality. Character could never be developed in such a place. All we have to do to rob our children of character is deprive them of struggle and endeavor. A God who would shut me away from all evil and clear my path of all sickness and trouble would rob me of the opportunity of character and morality. True character is always revealed by crisis.

Debate it all you wish. Spend a lifetime in study and research. Weigh the pros and cons of every theological lecture and sermon you have ever heard. It still comes down to a matter of faith. The real issue of faith will never be determined by the logic and verbal persuasion of man. God enters our darkness and pain and helps us to pray and often be comforted with groans and sighs that go beyond our words.

Ultimately, it is the *trustworthiness* of God that really matters. The object of Abraham's faith was not in what God had promised, although He desperately pursued the promises of God. His faith rested in God Himself.

I can never presume to answer the question *"Why, God?"* but I am finally at peace with the question, because my faith rests in God Himself.

Chapter 5

Living Without Wax

There are some in our world who can remember when "credibility was king," or a time when "a man's word was his bond." Today, unethical or controversial business activities often make headlines and are sadly described as "expected." There is no great surprise when government officials are called on the carpet for unethical acts. We've come to expect it. Recent events, however, have even rubbed the veneer off the surface of charities and some of our religious institutions. Many of our heroes have disappointed us. We have learned that the *super beings* have feet of clay. When they fail us, they lose our respect. The repetitive loss and corrosion of respect result in the loss of confidence.

No amount of success, rhetoric, public relation strategies, or image-building skills can ever gloss over the ugliness of a lack of ethics or integrity in the Christian life. If those who declare they are Christians are not believable, or if we advocate one thing and live another, it is doubtful that we will ever convince others to believe.

In Anne Tyler's novel, *Morgan's Passing,* the main character, Morgan Gower, runs a hardware store but often impersonates professionals, such as doctors, lawyers, counselors, or ministers. Being exposed, Morgan admitted, "It's all an image thing. You find out what people want and fit into it." Morgan realized that he could pretend to be many professions, but he also admitted that if he faked being a plumber or an electrician, he would be quickly found out because of his obvious lack of skills to solve the immediate crises.

The spiritual life is more than style, image, knowledge, technique and achievement. It is an expression of the integrity and the heart of God. My personal journey in the Christian life has been a consistent search for authenticity. Realness, substance, and significance are far more important than position or accolades. I believe there are many of you reading this book who share that search with me.

When I began writing this book, I never intended to make so many references to the life of Job. But it seems apparent that his struggle and character has imposed himself so much into my thought process that I can't ignore him. So, allow me once again to appeal to the judgment of a man who has come face to face with a test of personal integrity of enormous magnitude. In Job 31:6, Job concludes that it is better to be judged by God rather than man. He prays, "Let me be weighed on honest scales, that God may know my integrity" (NKJV).

This is both good and frightening. It's good because God knows. It's frightening because God knows. It is good if we are pure in our motives and intentions. It is frightening if we think God is going to be impressed by our PR releases or by our positions. It is good if our public and private lives are in agreement. It is frightening if there is any hint of duplicity in our lives because God knows.

Job further prays in verses 7-8, "If my step has turned from the way, or my heart walked after my eyes, or if any spot adheres to my hands, then let me sow, and another eat; Yes, let my harvest be rooted out"(NKJV). Basically, he is asking, *'God, have I strayed from your call? Have I veered off course? Have I gotten my eyes on the appearance of things rather than staying with the truth? Have I been influenced by the wrong motives, the wrong issues, or the wrong people?'*

One of the most heartwrenching, honest prayers of the Bible is recorded in verse 7. Job is really asking God for two things. First, he appeals to God to save his work, *'Let others benefit from what I have sowed.'* But, then Job prays, *'But if I have strayed from Your way, let my legacy be destroyed.'*

The Apostle Paul speaks to the church at Ephesus in Ephesians 4:1, "I, therefore, the prisoner of the Lord, beseech you to walk *worthy* of the calling with which you were called" (NKJV). Walking worthy of the call is to understand the word 'worthy'. Scales and weights were used in Paul's day to determine if something was deemed 'worthy' by virtue of its weight. The weightiness of God's calling cannot be matched by our *much doing.* We, as Christ followers and leaders, can never *do* enough, accomplish enough, nor perform in a worthy enough manner to be measured as worthy of God's call. Pretentious efforts are futile. Doing what God asks of us and doing it His way is the only manner in which the *scales* are reconciled or that we are able to walk worthy of our calling with which we are called. This does not look like the success that often receives the accolades of others.

When the Apostle Paul penned the book of Ephesians, there was no word in the Greek for 'worthy'. It was a concept that was untranslatable at the time Paul said it. So, Paul was instructing Christ-followers how to walk *worthy*. It had nothing to do with ceremony, ritual, nor good or bad circumstances, but had everything to do with humility, meekness, patience, forbearance as seen in the life and ministry of Jesus. These things are the opposite of pretense, masking, running ahead of God's wisdom, or self-seeking.

I believe the church is perhaps suffering more today from self-inflicted wounds than we are from external attacks.

I believe the church is perhaps suffering more today from self-inflicted wounds than we are from external attacks. Young people, and some not so young, are struggling with the question of authenticity. What is real and what is not real? What is for our gratification and what is for the glory of God? If we are to ever convince an unbelieving world to believe in Jesus Christ, we cannot preach and teach one thing and live by a different set of rules.

When we are honest with ourselves, then and only then will we face the myths we often use to justify doing or not doing certain things. Paul admonishes in 2 Corinthians 8:21, "For we are taking pains to do what is right, not only in the eyes of the Lord but also in the eyes of men" (NIV). For the Christian, ethics and integrity should always be routine and automatic. We shouldn't have to stop and think about it. No circumstances ever justify having to violate our own ethics or integrity.

The word "integrity" comes from the Latin word meaning "integer." It means to "bring the various parts into a whole or complete unit." We all have many components in each of our lives, and some of these are family, church, personal, social, professional, financial, and business. The process of bringing these areas together in godly arrangement is what Scripture calls *integrity*. Integrity declares that the whole is as important as each individual component.

The Bible says in Proverbs 11:3, "The integrity of the upright guides them, but the unfaithful are destroyed by their duplicity" (NIV). James declares in James 1:8, "A double-minded man is unstable in all his ways."

The Hebrew word "duplicity" used in Proverbs speaks of perverseness, distortion, and pretending to hold one feeling yet acting as if influenced by another. The Greek word for "double-minded" used in James is 'dipsuchos' and speaks of a man with two souls, one for earth and one for heaven. The inference is that the double-minded man alternates between his two souls. This, in essence, is a lack of integrity.

In January 2000, Commander Charles C. Crulack, USMC gave a speech at the Joint Services Conference on Professional Ethics. He told of an ancient Roman Army tradition that prevailed during the reign of twelve Caesars. Each morning, as an inspecting centurion would approach each legionnaire, the soldier would strike with his right hand the armor breastplate that covered his heart. He would then shout "integritas!" which means wholeness, completeness, and entirety. When the Imperial Army began its ascent to power and influence, the soldiers no longer cried "integritas" but began shouting "Hail Caesar" indicating that their hearts now belonged to the emperor, and no longer to one another or to a code of ideals.

For more than four centuries, the Romans successfully defended Rome against the Goths and Vandals. By 383 AD, the Barbarians were at the gate. Social decline in Rome had created lazy and negligent soldiers who had long since forgotten the ceremony of integrity, and had even convinced the emperor that it was no longer necessary to wear the heavy armor. They fought the Goths without protection of their hearts, and the arrows of the enemy found their target in the hearts of thousands of soldiers. Rome was defeated. Clearly, when one puts aside his or her integrity, the heart is always exposed to the enemy. It is no wonder that the Bible declares emphatically in Proverbs 4:23, "Above all else, guard your heart for everything you do flows from it" (NIV).

Christian integrity is not grounded on general themes or secular humanist ideals. Our integrity must be grounded on a fully integrated relationship with God. In order to have integrity in your walk, you must be honest with yourself and honest before God. Anything less is deceiving yourself. At best, our efforts to project a flawless image of ourselves is insincere. The prophet Jeremiah tells us, "The heart is deceitful above all things, and desperately wicked; who can know it?" (Jeremiah 17:9, NKJV) Those words of

Jeremiah are probably one of the reasons the Apostle Paul emphatically declared in 2 Corinthians 4:2, "We have renounced the hidden things of dishonesty, not walking in craftiness, nor handling the Word of God deceitfully."

A hurting soul is seen by some as evidence of spiritual immaturity or some heretical malady. That is probably why we Christians learn early how to pretend that we are okay even though we are deeply aware that we are not. We learn quickly to project an image that is not sincere. The words *sincere, sincerely* and *sincerity* are translated from words meaning *genuine, without deceit, unmixed* and *unadulterated*. The word "sincere" in English comes from two Latin words that mean literally "without wax" (John Ciardi, Browser's Dictionary and Native's Guide to the Unknown American Language, Harper & Row, New York, 1980, p. 360).

During the height of Roman and Greek artistry, sculpture became a popular artistic medium. When a sculpture had a flaw, artists would often fill in the chip or crack with colored wax to match the marble. Wax was said to serve as a cover-up, masking imperfections on what was most likely cheap pottery. An arguably perfect or quality piece of work was therefore *without wax*. Pottery pieces were even said to be stamped with the word "Sincere" or "Without Wax" as proof of authenticity.

In a similar fashion, it is easy to cover our character flaws and pretend or project that they are not there. That is insincere, lacking integrity and leading to the double-minded behavior of saying one thing and doing another.

Our true character is often revealed in the handling and coping of the trials we face. This should not frighten us. God often uses our trials to reveal our weaknesses and reveal to us how and what we need to overcome. In 1 Peter 4:12-13 the Apostle Peter lovingly wrote, "Beloved, do not think it strange concerning the fiery trial which is to try you, as though some strange thing happened to you; but rejoice to the extent that you partake of Christ's sufferings, that when His glory is revealed, you may also be glad with exceeding joy" (NKJV).

God allows the trials of our lives to act as fire to burn off the wax and expose our flaws and imperfections.

He allows the trials of our lives to act as fire to burn off the wax and expose our flaws and imperfections. The goal is not our destruction, but our integrity of walk. He allows trials so that through "the genuineness of your faith, being much more precious than gold that perishes, though it is tested by fire, may be found to praise, honor, and glory at the appearing of Jesus Christ" (1 Peter 1:7, NKJV).

David is a great example of this. David was a "man after God's own heart" and yet he spent over ten years running for his life and hiding from the murderous King Saul. In Psalm 13:1-4, David asks God, "How long, Lord? Will you forget me forever? How long will you hide your face from me? How long must I wrestle with my thoughts and day after day have sorrow in my heart? How long will my enemy triumph over me? Look on me and answer, Lord my God. Give light to my eyes, or I will sleep in death, and my enemy will say, 'I have overcome him,' and my foes will rejoice when I fall" (NIV).

Those are the sorrowful groanings of an aching heart that cannot understand what is happening to him. Yet, in the very next verses in Psalm 13:5-6, David recalls to mind the sincere integrity of his walk with God. This is where he makes a clear and bold declaration of faith that will help him stand. "But I trust in Your unfailing love; my heart rejoices in Your salvation. I will sing the Lord's praise, for He has been good to me" (NIV).

Unfortunately, even in Christian circles today, we seem to be surrounded by a conspiracy of pretense. As long as we are on this present earth, there is no way to escape the pain and suffering common to all humanity. The sooner we come to honest terms with that inescapable reality and quit trying to project that we are 'super saints', the sooner we can begin to have authenticity in our faith and in our daily walk.

Living a life of integrity does not negate the fact that we wrestle with the often unbearable, difficult issues of life. It does, however, bring us to place of trust in His great mercy and to the faith that undergirds us with strength to stand.

Chapter 6

Returning to Biblical Truth

Perhaps the greatest need of our time is that we get a clear picture of the real meaning of the Christian life. There is no guesswork in Christianity. God wants us to follow Him with eyes wide open to the expectations and to the challenges in following Christ in a fallen world.

Not everything which sounds Christian is indeed Christian. Very often myths, personal ideologies and popular tales parade as authentic Christian belief. Religious language with a smattering of scripture and a few testimonials are often misstated for truth. Theology has become, for many, a matter of personal opinion and has little to do with Biblical issues. When it is discussed, theology is so often presented in such abstraction as to have little to do with *real life.*

Have you ever wondered what Christianity would look like if every non-Biblical, man-made traditional trapping was stripped away? For centuries, believers have piled on their own misguided devotion, as well as those duly passed by denominational conferences. I guarantee you, Christianity would look very differently if we bypassed all of this and went straight back to the Bible.

This is not to suggest that tradition cannot be meaningful and have its place in the outworking of faith. The problem arises when those traditions that have been improperly imposed by men alter or even subvert basic, Biblical Christianity.

In his book, *When the Church Was Young*, originally published in 1935, Ernest Loosley declared that "When the church was young, it had no buildings, no denominations, no fixed organizations, no New Testament, no vocabulary of its own, no dogmatic system, and no day of Sabbath rest (in the Gentile World)." Loosley also states, "When the church was very young, it did possess an experience, a store of teaching from Christ, it had a gospel. The experience of the church was one the church knew it had to share. The church simply could do no other" (Edited & Revised by Christian Books Publishing Houses, Auburn, Maine, 1988).

The Apostles declared in Acts 4:20, "We cannot but speak the things which we have seen and heard" (NKJV). The church's store of teaching and experience was of such importance that the urge to spread it was irresistible. It was said of the early church in Acts 5:28, "You have filled Jerusalem with your teaching" (NIV).

There is a growing number of Christians who hunger for genuine Biblical Christianity. They desperately want to begin thinking more Biblically about God and how He responds to their needs, to their longings, and to them in a personal relationship. It is important to rid ourselves of pretense and get a firm grasp on true faith. Along with a growing multitude, I want to know God but not just about Him. Unless religion furnishes the consciousness with a right personal relationship with God, it will not satisfy the deepest longings of the human soul.

True Biblical Christianity believes solely what the Bible says about God, Jesus Christ, the Christian life and eternity.

True Biblical Christianity believes solely what the Bible says about God, Jesus Christ, the Christian life and eternity. There are no outside influences of man that affect the belief system of Christians. The Bible is our only source. The Christian God is personal. It is His Holy Spirit that communicates and interacts with mankind. He loves us even if we haven't loved Him. He wants us to know Him and have a personal relationship with Him.

There are some today who propose Christianity as a system of human reasoning which affirms *successful individuals* (whatever that means) as possessing the true essence of Christianity. But, the essence of Christianity is not in things. Some of the most dissatisfied people I know have a superabundance of things. People who have the means don't always have the meaning. The only thing which can truly satisfy a person is a harmonious relationship and fellowship with God. Jesus came to this earth to provide us with that opportunity. The Christian life is a life of right personal relationship of an individual with God through Jesus Christ. If God can equip us to live, to furnish us with faith, to overcome whatever obstacle we may face, He has met the fundamental need of our lives. This is what God is doing day by day. He is constantly seeking to give Himself. He will never withhold any good thing. He will never fail to do His part to maintain a life of fellowship. God is faithful.

I have often been troubled by some of our concepts of God's sporadic intervention in our lives, by the idea that He showed up "just in time." We seem to be able to relate to God only in those situations that seem fitting. We conveniently leave Him out of situations which don't fit our idea of those things in which a just God would be involved. The televised response of several of the recent hurricane victims brought this reality to mind. I listened as some who had escaped personal or property damage indicated they were spared by "the Hand of God." I listened to others who had lost most of their personal possessions and came close to losing their lives. I wondered how they felt they had been treated by God. It seems to be human nature to include God in the events that we consider positive and helpful, and to exclude Him when things are not so positive or considered good?

I recently saw a televised interview with two professional boxers. The winner was obviously ecstatic as he shouted into the microphone, "I want to thank my Lord Jesus Christ by helping me win this match tonight." The camera immediately focused on the other guy, who had been scrapped off the mat and was sitting on a corner stool with eyes swollen and was bleeding from both his nose and mouth. Sorry, but I couldn't help but wonder what this poor guy must be thinking about the "Lord Jesus Christ" if, in fact, God had helped with this severe beating he received. I don't know whether or not he was a believer. He never got a chance to say. If he was a Christian, I wonder if he would say, "I want to thank the Lord Jesus Christ for allowing me to get beaten up tonight." So much of what happens in our lives is because we are human. Being Christian does not exempt us from our humanness.

Whether our circumstances are good or whether they are bad, a Christian is never out of the reach of God's tender hands, and he is never out of view of God's compassionate eyes. The Bible tells us in Zechariah 4:10 that the "eyes of the Lord, which run to and fro through the whole earth." What an incredible picture. God loves us so much that He can't take His eyes off us!

There is an old saying that declares that a fish is the last to ask what water is. The Christian who has come to understand God's providence realizes that the only element in which we can survive is in God's wise and holy providence. Psalm 135:6 leaves no ambiguity about God's sovereignty. The Word declares, "Whatever the Lord pleases, He does, in heaven and in earth, in the seas and in all deep places" (NKJV). The simple truth is that we are not in charge. God is.

What about the idea of free will, you may ask? Free will does not suggest the presumptuous notion that we possess some natural liberty that allows us to choose all that happens in our lives and the consequences thereof. We have the ability to make choices freely, and we are responsible for all we do. But man is never able to make choices which conflict with facts clearly given to us in Scripture. It is by the act of our own will that we come to Christ. Then God wills that "as many as received Him, to them gave He power to become the sons of God, even to them that believe on His name" (John 1:12, NKJV).

If we are to have a God Whom we can worship, His character must be self-consistent and good. Otherwise, He would be a monster whom we might withdraw from in fear but whom we could never worship. In Jesus, God expressed Himself in human personality. Jesus did not sit in some ivory tower and hurl commands at His followers. The Bible says, "And being found in appearance as a man, he humbled himself and became obedient" (Philippians 2:8, NIV).

Jesus was the perfect model. He became a man and lived through every imaginable circumstance, being "tempted in all points" as we are. He demonstrated that relationship was a vital issue in surviving our humanity. He maintained a personal and momentous relationship with God and spent exhaustive efforts in establishing a consequential relationship with His disciples and others.

Authentic Biblical Christianity is distinguished from routine and ritualistic religion by an ever-increasing confidence that God is more than equal to the brokenness of our culture. True Christianity releases us from the bondage of our circumstances and frees us to receive the full assurance of a life sheltered in God's grace, sustained by the certainty of all that He has promised.

Because of Jesus' gift of life to us, we can stop pretending. He has secured for us what we could never secure for ourselves. Therefore, we are free to take off our masks and stop trying to earn our salvation. How liberating is that? We can now be real.

Living the Christian life isn't difficult. It is impossible. That is, it is impossible apart from a right relationship with God and the work of the Holy Spirit in our lives. To be truly led by the Spirit, we must be honest with God about what we are and Who He is.

Part 3:

Confident Living in Turbulent Times

Confidence is a strange thing. It can come, or it can go within a matter of minutes. One moment you may feel on top of the world and the master of your circumstances. Then something happens, and it seems as though your circumstances have ganged up on you, and the bottom has fallen out.

Of course, life does not always exist at a constant level of bliss. Circumstances change. We each experience our own mood swings. We find ourselves often having to wade through the murky uncertainties of day-to-day living. The loss of confidence is, however, much more serious. There is hardly anything more devastating to the human existence than to experience the searing pain of misplaced confidence and broken promises.

We have all experienced it. We each know what it is like to feel betrayed by someone we genuinely trusted. Sometimes people will let you down intentionally. Other times, it is done inadvertently because of unanticipated or uncontrollable circumstances. Either way, it hurts to be betrayed, especially if it is by a trusted friend or family member. Someone despondently remarked to me recently,

"It's gotten to where you don't know who you can trust."

Confidence brings with it assurance, hope and expectation. When it goes, it leaves behind smashed dreams and empty prospects. It is doubtful that any of us have escaped the debilitating loss of confidence, either within ourselves or in others. The question is *"Can God always be trusted?"*

A pastor recently told the story of a young gang member who was converted one week and asked to give a public testimony the next week. That can be dangerous. The young man began by telling how thankful he was to be a Christian. Then he told about how many times in his life he had been "sold down the river" by people in whom he had trusted. He concluded by admitting how happy he was to find Someone Who could be trusted. *"Nine times out of ten"* he proclaimed, *"you can trust God!"*

This was such a higher level of trust than he had ever experienced. He was ecstatic and probably thought that was as good at it gets. It isn't! If you can only trust God nine times out of ten, He isn't God. I really would not want to chance those odds, not with a God in Whom I have placed eternal hope. You can trust God ten times out of ten, one hundred times out of one hundred, a million times out of a million. He is God. He will fulfill what He has promised. We are in the covenant of His grace, and He holds back no good thing that He has promised. "No good thing will He withhold from them that walk uprightly. O Lord of Hosts, blessed is the man that trusteth in Thee" (Psalm 84:11-12).

Generally, where trust is mentioned in Scripture, it means to confide. So, to have confidence in God is to trust Him. It is exercising hope in God that He will be with us in all things and will carry us through, regardless of the circumstances. Confidence in God reflects assurance without arrogance. It demonstrates conviction tempered with humility and displays a courage that is constant, even in the face of discouraging circumstances.

Psalm 37:3 admonishes us to "Trust in the Lord, and do good; dwell in the land and feed on His faithfulness" (NKJV). Ephesians 3:12 tells us that it is through Christ our mediator, "In Him and through faith in Him we may approach God with freedom and confidence" (NIV). Paul declares in 2 Corinthians 3:4 "Such confidence as this is ours through Christ before God" (NIV).

We have accomplished so much that we believe in the primacy of the self to achieve whatever it wills.

North American Christianity seems to be suffering from its own success. We have accomplished so much that we have come to the place that we believe in the primacy of the self to achieve whatever it wills. Much teaching and preaching today seems to indicate that we can defeat any enemy and accomplish whatever we wish simply by putting an edge on our own skills and cunning. The problem is, if we trust in the power of human flesh, we will only get what flesh can deliver. If we arrive at that place of absolute trust in God, we will receive what He is able to bring about. God's antidote for fear, worry, and doubt is not strength but is confidence.

Confidence in God is not developed in a vacuum. It is developed by living constantly in the Presence of God. God Himself desires a personal and intimate relationship with each of us, and He has gone to great effort to assure that a relationship of this quality in attainable.

Living in the Presence of God is viewed historically as one of the deepest mysteries of the Christian faith. To fulfill this desire, many men and women have committed themselves to a monastic life, separating themselves from anyone or anything that may pose competition to their devotion to God. The idea is that if you meet the conditions for fellowship with God, you have your deepest need met. But, does living in God's Presence mean that we have to detach ourselves from living the normal, interactive life most of us are required to live in our present circumstances? Not at all. Living in His Presence means that we have come to understand the assertion of the Psalmist when he declares in Psalm 90:1, "Lord, Thou hast been our dwelling place in all generations."

In the vernacular of my understanding, a dwelling place is where you live, not some place that you occasionally visit. It is where you feel welcomed and comforted. It is where you feel loved and secure. Our bodies may reside in the most unpleasant of circumstances, but our souls and our inner beings are calmed in the Presence of the Lord.

Fundamental to any relationship is to keep putting ourselves in the presence of those with whom we desire fellowship. We stay in touch with friends and loved ones. Nothing is real to us which does not get our enduring attention. If we desire a meaningful relationship with God, we must acknowledge persistently that we are in the Presence of God. If we do not risk all in our fellowship with Him, we will never know the full joy of living in His Presence.

Any withholding will defeat the objective.

Living in His Presence provides us courage in the presence of our enemies, because we know we are never alone in our struggles. Living in His Presence furnishes hope in desperate situations, because we know that God is more than a match for any situation. Living in His Presence gives us confidence to face any circumstance, no matter how challenging.

Carved in Latin over the door of Carl Jung, Swiss psychiatrist who founded analytical psychology, are the words, "Bidden or not bidden, God is present." Although we know that God is always present in our lives, we must also realize there is a difference in Him being present and our having communion with Him. The spiritual presence of God in our lives is subject to our own spirituality. By His very nature, God cannot have communion with that which is not holy.

A. W. Tozer wrote: 'The Presence and the manifestation of the Presence are not the same. There can be the one without the other. God is here when we are wholly unaware of it. He is manifest only when and as we are aware of His presence. On our part, there must be surrender to the Spirit of God, for His is to show us the Father and the Son" (A. W. Tozer, *The Pursuit of God* (Christian Publications, Inc., Camp Hill, PA, 1982, 1993) p. 60).

Living in the Presence of God demands that we have awareness and a sense of awe in the face of God's holiness. That's not easy, and it is usually very threatening. The tension is real. We ask, *"How is it possible for sinful man to have fellowship with a holy God?"* Obviously, as we have learned from past experiences, we certainly can never attain through our own efforts that state of holiness necessary to have communion with God. We know that He is never going to lower His standards to have fellowship with sinful man. Herein is the most remarkable thing about the Christian faith. The believer has been elevated to communion with the Father through the Cross of Jesus Christ.

The most remarkable thing about the Christian faith is that the believer has been elevated to communion with the Father through the Cross of Jesus Christ.

Nicholas Herman (born about 1605 and better known as Brother Lawrence) wrote in a very aspiring way about prayer as consisting in a simple and constant practice of the Presence of God. He taught that, even amidst superficial affairs and daily occupations, it is possible to cultivate a life of contemplation. He insisted that every Christian has the ability, by the grace of God, to enjoy an ongoing fellowship with his Creator wherever he is and whatever he does.

Brother Lawrence said, "The Practice of the Presence of God is a way of life where we engage in continual conversation with God; walk with Him in love, humility, simplicity, and faith; and think, say, and do what is most pleasing to Him; because that is God's will for us." (http://www.thepracticeofthepresenceofgod.com)

When we are unaware of or we fail to acknowledge God's Presence, we allow our ears to become so filled with the backwash of human noises that the Voice of God is drowned out. If we are not hearing God's Voice progressively then we are not living in fellowship with Him. If we are not living in fellowship with Him, we will always be managed by our circumstances. It is by habitually hearing His Voice that we learn to hear it more clearly, and by hearing clearly, we follow.

God is always with us by His own promise. He proportions our trials and supplies us with grace and mercy for the occasion. God, who is always with us in tribulation, turns misery into mercy. When we acknowledge divine presence, our greatest trouble may become our highest advantage. The more we give ourselves to know God, the more He is able to make Himself known to us.

The best argument for Christianity is Christians. But, the strongest argument against Christianity is also Christians. Whether we like it or not, the whole Christianity community is under extreme scrutiny, perhaps as never before. That's okay. In fact, this is Christ's method. He said, "By this all will know that you are my disciples, if you have love for one another" (John 13:35, NKJV). Jesus invites the world to watch us.

There will come a time when your religion will fail you. God never will. Trust Him! Stay persistently in His Presence. Hear what He has said in His Word. See what He has done in the lives of others. Reflect on His dealings through the ages. Remember what He has done for you.

God is more than the sum total of everything, yet He is right here with us. He is closer to us than we are to ourselves. As Philip Yancey has observed, God seems to go where He's wanted.

Chapter 7

Beyond Superficial Religion

Have you ever asked yourself these questions:

- *What profit is there in serving God?*
- *Is there an absolute for human beings?*
- *Why should I be moral when those who don't seem to care about morality appear to be getting along as well, and sometimes better, than those who do?*

Those are the kinds of questions selfish logic asks. The Word of God, however, negates prideful human logic with the conclusion that there are questions far more important to ask. Such as:

- *Do I know what it is to live in the Presence of God?*
- *Do I have unrelenting confidence that God is with me, and that He will never leave me?*
- *Do I understand the relational aspect of Christianity?*

- *Do I have a calm assurance that my circumstances will not prevail, but my faith in God will?*
- *Have I developed a faith to stand, even when I can't understand my circumstances?*

The Christian life is about more than religion, chaos and utter spontaneity. It is about closeness, connection and relationship. It is about God who becomes flesh like us so we may understand His plans for us and experience His love and enjoy fellowship with Him. Because we live in the proper relationship with God, we are also learning daily how to live in relationship with one another. One cannot be a Christian without expressing his or her life in relationships.

I have read many of the books which attempt to answer some of the tough questions about God and His dealings with mankind, but most of them left me with a deep, sinking feeling that all God did was to get creation off to a reasonably good start, and then He disappeared. I know better. I know that God is continuing to reveal Himself in our lives in ways which are nothing short of supernatural.

I've given up attempting to answer all the questions. What I have come to understand is that when people raise questions about God and suffering, these are usually cries of pain, not appeals for some theological discourse. What suffering people need usually is compassion, not answers. We all can give compassion. There is a time and place for advice and answers, but it is not when a person is going under for the third time. Christianity is not good advice. It is *Good News*.

I recently heard of a little girl who told her psychologist father that she helped a friend at school whose father had just died. Curious to know which of his techniques his daughter had learned and employed, her father asked, *"What did you say and what method did you use?"*

"I didn't know what to say." replied his daughter. *"So, I just sat down and cried with her."*

Obviously, there are times when a crisis is so acute that intervention might be required. I am in no way implying to oversimplify nor minimize the value of clinical or theological resources. In fact, I wholeheartedly embrace intercessory prayer, interpersonal support, pastoral care, worship, sacraments, and community as keys to healing and wholeness.

What I am suggesting is that oftentimes all we need is someone to truly care. Oftentimes, what we long for is someone who is more interested in us than in a learned method or technique. We need someone who will readily admit they cannot 'fix' everything, but will cry with us in our time of distress. This is the reason we are exhorted in Romans 12:15 to "Rejoice with those who rejoice and weep with those who weep."

What is true? Who can I believe? How can I be sure I'm right? What if I'm wrong, not just in the insignificant matters but where it really counts? Can I ever truly settle all the questions and doubts, or is it a lifetime challenge?

We have been taught that it is inadmissible to raise such questions, but a faith that has never been challenged, never tested and never questioned is a fragile faith, a faith which has little chance of surviving critical times. The Psalmist knew the importance of being tested as he reveals in Psalm 139:23-24, "Search me, O God, and know my heart: try me, and know my thoughts: And see if there be any wicked way in me, and lead me in the way everlasting."

Show me the person who has never questioned his or her faith, and I'll show you a person whose faith has not been tried in the crucible.

Show me the person who has never questioned his or her faith, and I'll show you a person whose faith has not been tried in the crucible of unexplainable suffering or sorrow. On the other hand, show me the individual who has been wrestled to the mat by intimidating circumstances and has climbed to his or her feet to embrace faith, and I'll show you a person who knows the real meaning of faith.

In times such as these, it is essential that we are confident regarding the certainties of the Christian faith. It is time for Christians to stop exerting so much energy over nonessentials. It is time to stop wandering in the wilderness of dried-up experiences and scratching in the cold ashes of yesterday's revival in an attempt to reignite the passion. It is time that we stop debating techniques and methods and get on with fulfilling our purpose and mission on earth. We spend too much time trying to discover the patterns of yesterday's experiences, when God desires to create a new thing among us. We are often too fast to soar and too slow to anchor. We must find firm ground to stand on. We can't afford to fake it. There is too much at stake.

It's doubtful that any of us can honestly say that we have arrived at that place of calm assurance for which we strive. Fritz Ridenour defines Christians "as the 'not-yet-ones', always pressing onward, not quite finished, but looking forward to a state of glory that is beyond imagining." He says, "Truly, we are in God's process and His goal for us is that we be perfect -- whole, complete, mature -- *grown up!* And what of our failures? We welcome them as a way to grow. For the not-yet-ones, failure always leads toward eventual success. We have already overcome the world by placing our faith in Christ. We continue to overcome as we obey, love and believe" (Fritz Ridenour, *How To Be A Christian Without Being Perfect* (Ventura, California: Regal Books, 1986) pp.169-170).

Undoubtedly, this is what Paul meant when he said in Philippians 3:13-14, "Brethren, I do not count myself to have apprehended; but one thing I do, forgetting those things which are behind and reaching forward to those things which are ahead, I press toward the goal for the prize of the upward call of God in Christ Jesus" (NKJV).

There is a great "cloud of witnesses" which surrounds us. These are those who have made it. They know the struggles. They know the sacrifices. They know the setbacks the Christian may suffer. Listen closely, however, and you will hear their words through the move of the Holy Spirit say to you, *"Go on!" "You can make it." "It is worth it!"*

Chapter 8

Beyond Blind Optimism

Nowhere in Scripture are we encouraged to view Christianity as a means which allows us to simply "look on the bright side" of our situation. There are no magic formulas promised. Christianity is a relationship and can never be understood through any other process. To be a Christian is to be rightly related to God and to live in supportive relationships with one another. To be a Christian is to embrace hope that goes beyond mere optimism and wishful thinking to discover a calm assurance that reflects confidence in promises *guaranteed* by God Himself.

In discussing some of the issues confronting our society and especially the church, I recently asked a friend if he was optimistic or pessimistic. *"Neither,"* he replied. *"I'm hopeful."*

Good answer. It is one with which I relate. Few of us can identify with the artificial optimism which exudes from some Christian leaders. It sounds so phony. Sometimes you feel like standing up and shouting, *"You apparently haven't been living on my block!"* But, none of us can continually tolerate the acidic pessimism which is dispensed by those terminally morbid souls who promise nothing but gloom and doom and despair. Pessimism can be debilitating. False optimism can be fatal. Thankfully, Christians don't have to wallow in either of these philosophies. We are the only people on earth who have any foundation or any right to hope. Everything else is either wishful thinking or fatalistic speculation.

Christians are the only people who have any foundation or any right to hope. Everything else is either wishful thinking or fatalistic speculation.

We are eye witnesses to a society on the edge of despair. It's unlikely that any of us have been unaware of the devastating hopelessness into which many have fallen, and it hasn't been without cause. Our civilization has been in radical tumult for the past several years. We've seen our political institutions degenerate. Our religious organizations have faltered. Our educational institutions have failed in their original purposes. We keep thinking there is some political or religious leader who will lead us out of the morass. We listen to their promises, but we doubt their sincerity and ability to change things. Those who promise to help seem to be getting us deeper into the quagmire. Is it any wonder that so many people have such a dark, pessimistic outlook for the future?

Earlier in this book, I warned about the false advertisement of religion. Now I want to focus on the other side of that issue and suggest that the greatest problem for some is not that the Gospel is being overstated, but that it is being understated. We should never be afraid to confess all that Christ has offered in the Gospel, but there is never any reason for us to promise more than God has promised. The Gospel is sufficient. It is the only message that will provide hope to an otherwise hopeless generation. No other individual or movement or organization can ever be the hero of the Gospel. Jesus Christ is the hero of the Gospel. He is the only hero.

Christians, especially evangelicals, are constantly being redefined by the uninformed media. Often, the way we are being defined by some of our own doesn't give us a much better clue as to who we are. A tremendous confidence surfaces when you allow the Bible to define who you are in relation to God rather than letting the world define who you are in relation to groups and organizations.

The Christian hope is not a trembling, hesitant hope projecting that perhaps the promises of God *might* be true or, at least, some of them *might* be trustworthy. It is the confident expectation that cannot be anything else but true. It's not taking a chance or weighing our options. Christian hope, as defined by J. I. Packer, is the "guaranteed, never-ending generosity of God."

The writer of Hebrews says, "This hope we have as an anchor of the soul, both sure and steadfast" (Hebrews 6:19, NKJV). Purveyors of hopelessness dismiss these words as exaggeration and choose to live in despair. But the Christian receives them as absolute Truth and realizes that we are never beyond the reach of God's great hope through Jesus Christ.

Even as you read these words, Satan may be telling you that God has made promises that haven't been fulfilled. If so, rely on that light of hope which God has ignited within you. Perhaps it seems to be only a 'pilot light' at this time. Fuel it by rehearsing what God has already done for you. Fuel it with what He has promised you in His Word. When you do, God's Holy Spirit stirs up the embers within you and faith arises in your spirit. Then that fire will burst into a glowing, warming flame by which you and others may be comforted and find hope in His Presence.

Satan can defeat the frantic believer, but he is never a match for those who calmly rest their hopes in the assurance of God's promises and purposes. Not only does Christianity offer us hope for the here and now, but it prepares us for eternity. And we must never neglect that transcendent Truth.

I had just finished speaking to a group of students at a Christian rally on the campus of Louisiana State University, and I honestly felt good about what I had said that night. I felt especially good about those who came forward for prayer. Several students to the left of the platform motioned for me, so I walked over to where they were.

One of the students spoke for the small group. *"When you began speaking tonight, we thought we were going to enjoy your message,"* she said. That's not the most encouraging thing for a speaker to hear, but I, at least, respected their honesty.

"What did I say that changed your mind?" I asked.

"Well, you began by talking about current and relevant things -- things we are interested in. But you ended up like most other preachers, talking about 'pie in the sky in the sweet by and by'. We're not interested in the hereafter. We want to know about the here and now."

To tell you the truth, it stung, and I felt the sting for several days. I could hardly get the statement off my mind: *"We liked you when you began, but you ended up like the rest."*

As I remember it, I had actually said very little about eternity that night, but it obviously raised passionate questions, to at least a few, as to my relevance. The incident caused me to ask some earnest questions about my preaching. Since most of my ministry had been to young people, I had always thought I was contemporary. But now, I had been told otherwise.

What relevance does the hereafter have on the here and now? Everything. I believe in the present. I understand the importance of being relevant and up-to-date. I understand that we live out the crucibles of everyday life here on earth. However, a faith which does not have eternity as a cornerstone is frail and seriously flawed.

If it is true that we humans possess a kind of appetite for eternity as revealed in most religions, including pagan religions, this generation seems to be caught up in ventures which frustrate that desire. We seem to be content to live for the present and let the future take care of itself. But we are not, nor can we ever truly be, temporal creatures. We are created for eternity.

St. Augustine, one of the early church fathers, said in his Confessions, "You have made us and drawn us to yourself, and our heart is unquiet until it rests in you." Indeed, we were made for Him and by Him, and our hearts will always be restless until we find full rest in Him.

Unless you want to stagger through the gloom of a senseless existence, you had better restore your faith in eternity. Without an understanding of what God has in mind for our future, few things in this life make any sense to the Christian. The Bible says in 1 Corinthians 15:19, "If in this life only we have hope in Christ, we are of all men the most pitiable" (NKJV).

In his book, *Man's Search For Meaning,* Viktor Frankl gives a moving account of his life amid the horrors of the Nazi death camps. As a prisoner in Auschwitz and other concentration camps, Frankl watched the Nazis attempt to dehumanize men and women. According to his report, those who survived were those who gained inner strength through some future goal. Survival meant living beyond the here and now.

Frankl says "It is a peculiarity of man that he can only live by looking to the future -- *sub specie aeternitatis.* And this is his salvation in the most difficult moments of his existence, although he sometimes has to force his mind to the task" (Viktor Frankl, *Man's Search For Meaning* (New York: Touchstone Books, 1984) p. 58).

The Christian has many blessings and undeniable benefits in this life, but our real hope is beyond the grave. This future hope is the inspiration of present faith and love. It was because of their hope in the resurrection that the early Christians suffered persecution. No truth more infuriates Satan. Why? Because he knows that a genuine future hope is a strong motivation for living for Christ in the here and now.

Most of the pleasures of this earth are light-winged and illusive. They disappear in the drought of summer and in the cold winds of winter. But the Christian's hope is strong and lofty and will survive the severest trial. Our hope never resides with objects, environment or circumstances. Our hope is fulfilled in Him in Whom we have believed. I have not always been able to rejoice in my circumstances, but I have always been able to rejoice in the Lord.

There are no hopeless situations, only hopeless people. They wait for someone to point them toward genuine hope. Only Christians have such hope.

Chapter 9

Beyond Circumstance
and Cynicism

The Christian race is a marathon. It is not a hundred-yard
dash. At no point along the way will Satan give up on trying
to confuse you, kill your faith and destroy your joy. He will harass
you to the finish. He doesn't mind that you still go to church or
that you still profess to know Jesus Christ. He doesn't even mind
that you hold on to the ceremony of religious formulas and rituals.
What Satan wants is to have your confidence in God so shaken
by baffling occurrences and by overpowering circumstances that
confidence gives into uncertainty.

Hopefully, there are some things we have learned at this point in
our journey. For one thing, we should have learned by now that our
sweet sounding religious clichés are not going to rescue us from the
clutches of living as a human being in a sinful environment. We should
know by now that an abundance of things will not bring satisfaction.

Each of us must find an "ought" within us which propels us to continue our Christian journey, in spite of the difficulties and setbacks we may face. Faith to stand brings with it full assurance that our trust in God will carry us through, even when we can't make sense of the circumstances.

Trouble is a constant shadow. You can't run fast enough to stay ahead of it. You can't hide from it. You can't escape it. Trouble will find you. Trouble is no respecter of persons. In times of trouble, we either move toward God or away from Him.

It is a mistake to think that all trouble is an accident. It is often the enduring of trouble that molds us into the person God has in mind for us to become. It is tribulation which often opens to us the true meaning of Scripture. Check your own Bible, the one you use for personal devotions, and you are likely to find that many of the highlighted or underlined verses are those which were marked during the midst of a trial. At least, it is so with me. Don't worry that your troubles will be too much and will last too long. God knows how much you can bear. He knows how much you need to bear. The end result will always bring glory to God.

James 1:2-4 says, "Consider it pure joy, my brothers, whenever you face trials of many kinds, because you know that the testing of your faith develops perseverance. Perseverance must finish its work so that you may be mature and complete, not lacking anything" (NIV). Paul, weighted down under a heavy burden, declared, "Indeed, in our hearts we felt the sentence of death. But this happened that we might not rely on ourselves but on God, who raises the dead" (2 Corinthians 1:9, NIV).

The idea that becoming a Christian clears one's path of all difficulty, conflict and adversity did not originate with Scripture.

The idea that becoming a Christian clears one's path of all difficulty, conflict and adversity did not originate with Scripture. In fact, the Apostle Paul affirms the opposite. He says "All that live godly in Christ Jesus will suffer persecution" (2 Timothy 3:12). You can count on it. As long as you live, breathe and have an earthly address, Christian or not, you will face adversity.

In his second letter to Timothy, Paul assures his young friend that believers will face "perilous days" which will test the faith of the most earnest soul. Paul's admonition to Timothy is to "continue in the things which you have learned and been assured of, knowing from whom you have learned them" (2 Timothy 3:14, NKJV).

There are two crucial questions in this admonition. First, can you trust the things you have learned? Second, do you trust the people who taught you?

The Greek word Paul used for "perilous" literally means "evil," "demonic," or "lion like." It bears a striking similarity to what the Bible says about Satan in 1 Peter 5:8, "Be sober, be vigilant; because your adversary the devil walks about like a roaring lion, seeking whom he may devour" (NKJV).

The word "perilous" focuses on the idea of reducing one's strength so that he or she becomes vulnerable to the dangers of evil. By implication, Paul is telling Timothy to take precaution not to allow his faith to be weakened by the things he sees or experiences.

We cannot determine to avoid the bitter experiences of pain, suffering, grief and separation common to all humans, but we can determine how we will respond to them. After learning that she had cancer, Shelley Chapin declared, "God is completely trustworthy, and He does not lose His will, His plan, or His people in the midst of the storm. Central to His very character is the faithful, unchanging quality that causes demons to tremble at the mention of His name" (Shelley Chapin, *Within The Shadow* (Wheaton IL: Victor Books, 1991) p. 18).

To ministers, Chapin says, "First of all, realize that it is not your job to alter circumstances. It is the minister's job to love and to reflect the brilliant nature of God in otherwise bad situations" (p. 151).

Pastor Ron Mehl, after learning that he had leukemia, wrote a book entitled *Surprise Endings* in which he declares, "Life isn't a rose garden, and none of us have been promised that. . . James says maturity and spiritual growth come from letting patience have her perfect work, testing every virtue and challenging every weakness. Patience makes a trip around our life and looks for any weaknesses and flaws. No mature saint can say that his stature in Christ has come without tribulations and trials and agony over delays and prayers that seem to go unanswered" (Ron Mehl, *Surprise Endings* (Sisters, Oregon: Multnomah, 1993) p. 139).

There is much I don't understand about suffering, but some things I do know. I know that suffering has been part of the human experience since man's fall into sin. At least one third of the Psalms are laments which portray the reality of human suffering. The theme of the Book of Job (here I go with Job again) is the problem of suffering and why God permits the righteous to suffer.

Whatever the Lord allows us to experience in life is a developing experience to help us in our goal of becoming more like Jesus. If we are not becoming more like Him, there is a disconnect. The Bible says that Jesus was perfected through suffering. Hebrews 2:10 declares, "For it was fitting for Him, for whom are all things and by whom are all things, in bringing many sons to glory, to make the captain of their salvation perfect through sufferings" (NKJV).

Those who suffer are in a position to comfort others. 2 Corinthians 1:3-6 proclaims, "Blessed be the God and Father of our Lord Jesus Christ, the Father of mercies and God of all comfort, who comforts us in all our tribulation, that we may be able to comfort those who are in any trouble, with the comfort with which we ourselves are comforted by God. For as the sufferings of Christ abound in us, so our consolation also abounds through Christ. Now if we are afflicted, it is for your consolation and salvation, which is effective for enduring the same sufferings which we also suffer. Or if we are comforted, it is for your consolation and salvation" (NKJV).

Paul admonished Timothy in 2 Timothy 1:6, "Wherefore I put thee in remembrance that thou stir up the gift of God, which is in thee by the putting on of my hands." Timothy is the pastor of the church in Ephesus and undoubtedly recognizes that the directives of this word from his mentor are to be taken seriously. The word here translated "stir up" literally means to rekindle. Paul seems to be saying, *"I sense that you are in great danger of losing your zeal. I realize how greatly you are tempted to allow the fire to go out on the altars of your soul. Rekindle the gift of God that is within you."*

Paul is not accusing Timothy of having put out his fire. He did not say, "Stop pouring water on your fire." He didn't say, "You're smothering your fire." In order for a fire to go out, it is not necessary that it always be put out. All that is necessary is to ignore it, and it will go out for the lack of attention.

Paul is not trying to instill in Timothy some new idea, nor is he urging him to acquire new gifts. He is not pushing him to use some gift that he doesn't possess. He is not saying you have to lead with the skills of another or demonstrate gifts of another. Paul is simply saying "don't let die what God has given you."

It isn't necessary for a man or woman to fall into open sin in order to nullify the effect of their Christian testimony. All they have to do is to lose their passion and devotion for Christ. Old habits continue for a season, but they are soon lost in the ritual of performance. The loss of passion in ministry is one of the greatest dangers the church faces today.

There are enemies in this war for your confident trust in God. If you are not vigilant, they will rob you of passion for living in the Presence of God. Some key indicators of waning passion are:

- **Losing sight of what God has done in your life.** Before you can "stir up" the gift, you must recognize that you have such a gift. Embrace God's call, and celebrate all of the magnificent things He has done in your life. Remember where you were when He found you and where you would be without Him.

    2 Timothy 1:6-7 "Therefore, I remind you to stir up the gift of God which is in you through the laying on of my hands. For God has not given us

a spirit of fear, but of power and of love and of a sound mind" (NKJV).

Hebrews 2:1 "Therefore, we ought to give the more earnest heed to the things which we have heard, lest at any time we should let them slip."

- **Neglecting personal devotions.** Fail to give yourself to the Word of God and to prayer, and the fire will die. Loyalty and devotion are at the very heart of the Christian's faith. And this loyalty and devotion must be constantly kindled afresh to keep the fire hot, the flames high, and the coals glowing.

1 Thessalonians 4:1 "Finally, dear brothers and sisters, we urge you in the name of the Lord Jesus to live in a way that pleases God, as we have taught you. You are doing this already, and we encourage you to do so more and more" (NLT).

- **Focusing on Self.** It never fails. When members of the Body of Christ decide that they are going to do their own thing and neglect the interdependency that God has in mind for His Church, the passion soon fades into shades of egotism and self-centeredness, and the anointing is forfeited.

Philippians 1:9 "My prayer for you is that you will overflow more and more with love for others, and at the same time keep on growing in spiritual knowledge in insight" (TLB).

Philippians 2:3 "Let nothing be done through strife or vainglory, but in lowliness of mind let each esteem other better than themselves."

- **Submitting to the three terrible R's of traditionalism.** In *Word Pictures in The New Testament, Vol. I*, Dr. A.T. Robertson writes of the three terrible R's of traditionalism. What are they?
  - **Rote:** Repetition carried out mechanically or unthinkingly.
  - **Rut:** Walking the well-worn paths from one event to another. Someone has defined a rut as a grave with both ends knocked out. God occasionally wants us to blaze some new trails.
  - **Rot:** The inevitable end of rote and rut is Rot. When the spring ceases to flow, it stagnates. The moment you and I cease to grow spiritually, we begin to die.

    Colossians 1:10 "And we pray this in order that you may live a life worthy of the Lord and may please Him in every way: bearing fruit in every good work, growing in the knowledge of God" (NIV).

- **Falling Prey to Cynicism.** *The Oxford English Dictionary* describes a cynic as a person "disposed to rail or find fault" and as one who "shows a disposition to disbelieve in the sincerity or goodness of human motives and actions, and is wont to express this by sneers and sarcasm." In short, the cynic is "a sneering fault-finder." Cynicism, while aimed at pouring water on the flame of another, usually quenches the fire of the one holding the water bucket.

    1 John 4:11 "Dear friends, since God loved us that much, we surely ought to love each other" (NLT).

    Matthew 7:3-4 "Why do you look at the speck of

sawdust in your brother's eye and pay no attention to the plank in your own eye? How can you
say to your brother, 'Let me take the speck out
of your eye,' when all the time there is a plank in
your own eye?" (NIV)

This is no pie-in-the-sky story. The Christian life is difficult.
There's no easy passage from our first experience of God's love to
that final reward of entrance into heaven. It is a journey with many
challenges, ups and downs. There are obstacles and temptations at
every turn. But, there is also incredible help along the way. Jesus
told us in John 14:26 that, "the Holy Spirit, whom the Father will
send in My Name, will teach you all things and will remind you of
everything I have said to you" (NKJV).

I don't know where you are in your Christian journey. The question isn't '*How long have you been on this journey?*' The important
questions are, '*Are you still making progress?*' and '*Are you growing
up in all things into Him?*'

Even though there will be bumps and bruises throughout the
believer's life, Jesus Christ has promised to be with us until the end,
as recorded in Matthew 28:19, 20; "Go therefore and make disciples
of all the nations, baptizing them in the name of the Father and of
the Son and of the Holy Spirit, teaching them to observe all things
that I have commanded you; and lo, I am with you always, even to
the end of the age. Amen" (NIV).

The journey is gloriously and eternally worthwhile!

Conclusion

Circumstances often seem to conspire with Satan to keep us from maintaining our resolve to trust God, regardless. Simple trust seems to be out of fashion today. Self-protection and pretension have become the norm. We have become very adept at innovating strategies and formulas to help us climb out of our circumstances. It is tempting to distance ourselves from problems for which there are no easy answers. We don't like to admit that we are totally dependent upon resources beyond our control.

But that is exactly what authentic Christianity teaches; to be utterly dependent on God and to trust all His ways. Proverbs 3: 5,6 "Trust in the Lord with all your heart, and lean not on your own understanding. In all your ways acknowledge Him, And He will direct your paths" (NKJV). We cannot pick ourselves up by our own bootstraps, change our circumstances by pretending, or simply attempting to revise our perspective. Hope comes as a result of learning to trust that God is in charge, and that He will provide whatever we need to make it through.

'We live in a fallen world' is a statement we often make and hear others say in response to questions of why some tragic event has taken place. But, do we truly realize how powerful that statement is? Allow me to position that question in its appropriate context. We hear the phrase *fallen world*, and our minds are appropriately drawn to the images and Scriptures about the Garden of Eden as described in Genesis. This was the world before God's creation was *fallen*.

It was glorious beyond description, but then Lucifer, the outcast father of lies, slithered his way into the minds and hearts of Adam and Eve. We see the sharp contrast of a world glorious beyond our understanding with the image of Adam and Eve hiding from God as He calls their names. They ran as God expelled them from the perfect Garden He had created for them. It was then that all of creation began groaning and longing for the appearing of Hope and Redemption.

Adam and Eve began living in the *fallen world* with all its consequences, and so it would continue for all people throughout the generations until the Messiah came to live among His creation. Adam and Eve would experience the birth and death of their son, disease, harvests that did not come easily, threatening forces of nature, and the sacrifice of animals to a God that no longer walked with them in the cool of the day. The sorrow and shock of the series of events in their lives in contrast with the life they knew in the Garden of Eden was, to say the least, beyond comprehension.

The concept of *fallenness* could not possibly have been understood exhaustively by the generations of Adam. It wasn't until the time of the prophets, such as Isaiah, that God began to reveal a Promise given that would change everything about the fallen nature of man.

The prophet Isaiah proclaimed a Promise of Redemption and Hope that seldom comes to our mind when we experience trials that are overwhelming. More often than not, we turn to the Psalms during those times, and rightfully, we should. We seek out Scriptures that speak of God's trustworthiness when unspeakable doubts and fears assault our faith. Trusting God is found in unbendable, unshakable, undeniable faith. That kind of deep faith comes through an understanding of Who God is through Jesus Christ, and what Christ did to reconcile and offer redemption to every person that has and will ever live on this earth.

Trusting God is found in unbendable, unshakable, undeniable faith that comes through understanding Who God is, and what Jesus Christ did to reconcile and redeem every person.

The Messianic prophecy in Isaiah 9:6-7 is important for today and not just during our Christmas celebrations: "For unto us a Child is born, unto us a Son is given; And the government will be upon His shoulder. And His name will be called Wonderful, Counselor, Mighty God, Everlasting Father, Prince of Peace. Of the increase of His government and peace there will be no end. Upon the throne of David and over and His Kingdom. To order it and establish it with judgment and justice from that time forward, even forever.

The zeal of the Lord of hosts will perform it" (NKJV).

What a marvelous Scripture of promise that changes everything about fallen mankind, if we have faith to believe it! In the dark circumstances of your life, does the response of Christ always seem to show Him as *Wonderful?* Does He seem to answer every situation with perfect understanding as a great *Counselor?* Can you recall times that you prayed fervently because you knew only a *Mighty God* could prevent a certain thing from occurring, but He didn't seem to answer?

How often do we hear someone say, 'How can I believe in a good, *Everlasting Father?* I've never known a good father that even showed up when I needed him, so how can I trust a father that is supposedly everlasting?'

Many people laugh in your face when you speak about peace. They might say, "Look around. Do you see anything that remotely appears to be real peace, much less the existence of an everlasting *Prince of Peace?"*

It is in these times when we hear these haunting fears and doubts about the God we serve that we realize, oftentimes, our answers are just not enough. We must live out of the Truth that God has declared of Himself in His Word and through the life of Jesus Christ, regardless of how the circumstances of life appear.

God's Word, spoken through the prophet Isaiah, foretold Who Jesus was, Who He is today, and that He will fulfill every promise spoken of Who He is in the future. He is, was, and will always be Wonderful above all gods. Our compassionate, wise, and just Counselor will never tire of His children's words and will respond to their cries for His help as they call on Him. He will always hear. He will always be a Counselor of Truth that can be trusted.

Our Mighty, all-powerful God is also our always-attentive, faithful Everlasting Father. He is our Abba Father. Jesus Christ, the Prince of Peace, was born in the humblest of conditions and lived as our example in and through all life's circumstances. He died as the Spotless Lamb of God Who was the ultimate, sufficient sacrifice for our Sin. And, because He was resurrected, He is the Conqueror of death, Hell, and the grave, and promises to return as the King of Kings and the Lord of Lords. He will usher His children and all of mankind into the justice, glory and unspeakable beauty for all eternity, just as He promised through Isaiah centuries before.

Finding the faith to stand comes through the assurance there will be no end to His righteous reign.

Finding the faith to stand comes through the assurance there will be no end to His righteous reign. Justice will be the last thing to be explained and understood. There will be a final Judgment. There will be a time that all tears will be wiped from our eyes. There will be a time that we no longer see through a glass dimly and will understand all the circumstances that have taken place over the course of our lives.

We must resist the efforts to make this Gospel of Jesus Christ void of sorrow and pain, in an effort to make it palpable to a watching world. It's not all about the here and now. We are truly the 'not-yet-ones'. In the vast sea of sorrowfulness, it is difficult to see beyond the floundering of our own little boat, but we must realize that our sunsets always flow into God's horizons.

I can now look back on my most painful and devastating experiences with fulfillment. Most of what I have truly learned in life is not associated with the fleeting phantom called happiness, but has come through affliction and sorrow. I could not have said this a few years ago. But, now I know that these experiences are paramount to my being. If it were possible to eliminate all afflictions from my life, I would choose not to do it. I fear that in so doing, it would make life so trivial and meaningless that it would not be worth living.

Jesus could have certainly avoided the Cross, but where would that have left us? It is His willingness to submit completely to the will of God, including the suffering of the Cross that inevitably draws men and women to Him.

The valuable legacy of sorrow is that it leaves us the richer for having experienced it. While it is true that we never quite get over the sorrow caused by the loss of those whom we love the most, it makes living a richer thing. The grief process leads to a path of greater understanding and to personal renewal while preserving the meaning of life and the person we have lost. I have often heard it said that it is the bad times that make people appreciate the good times. But for me, the difficult times that I have experienced make me appreciate the *ordinary* ones.

Obviously, we will never fully understand the purpose for our trials and struggles until we are with Him in eternity. We do know, however, that He loves us far too much to harm us. In fact, He is far more concerned with our welfare than we are. His choices are always accurate. If He is indeed sovereign, then nothing in His universe happens by chance or accident. For every effect, there is a cause. Paul reminds us in Ephesians 1:11, 12 "(God) worketh all things after the counsel of His own will: That we should be to the praise of His glory."

The Christian life is not a set of rules, regulations or magic formulas. When it comes right down to it, the only thing we have in this life that cannot be taken from us by tragedy, death or by a court of law is Jesus Christ. When we finally come to the end of our strength and fictitious rituals and realize that Jesus is The Way, The Truth and The Life, we will have discovered the genuine meaning of what it means to be a Christian, and what it means to live confidently in Him. In Jesus' Kingdom, there are not the blessed and the unblessed. In His Kingdom, there are not winners and losers. All will "win the prize for which God has called me (us) heavenward in Christ Jesus" (Philippians 3:14, NIV).

Hebrews chapter eleven introduces an amazing group of people with an incredible array of personalities. When you look at the list, you see a scattered community of strangers, exiles, underdogs – all of them unexpected heroes of the faith. Look closely at their lives that God caused to be changed.

- Noah: By the definition of some, he was a drunken sailor and was disgraced.
- Abraham: A pilgrim who resorted to a lie to accomplish his destination to a land where God told him to go.
- Sarah: A jealous, scheming wife who felt she needed to orchestrate God's promise.
- Moses: A murderer who took matters into his own hands

to retaliate against the enemy of God's people.

- Rahab: A harlot who hid the men of God.

These are names most of us recognize. When reading this chapter, you will quickly discover that many names are missing from the list of heroes. The passage that stands out for me consists of two words in verse 36, "AND OTHERS." The writer seems to be saying, *'I could go on, but you get the idea. God has many heroes of the faith, and most of them remain unnamed.'*

What one discovers in reading this chapter is that Bible heroes were just ordinary people who God chose to use for extraordinary purposes. Most of them were definitely not number one draft choices. Yet, from a more important view, they became living hope. They were in tune with God's biggest hopes for the human family. They lived out their lives in ways that revealed God's faithfulness to them. It also assures us that God is equally as faithful to us today.

The whole point of Hebrews 11 is that God can take what we place in His hands and create something of infinite value. The secret of those "heroes of the faith," and the one thing we all have in common are both found in the first two verses of the eleventh chapter of Hebrews. "To have faith is to be sure of the things we hope for, to be certain of the things we cannot see. It was by their faith that people of ancient times won God's approval" (GNT).

The Christian life requires more than prudence, simply possessing some gift of far-sightedness. Prudence contemplates what can be perceived with the senses. Faith, according to Hebrews 11:1, means being certain of what is not yet seen. Because we are physical beings living in a spiritual world, we need faith as a navigational aid. It's trusting entirely in God's calling and in His ability and willingness to equip us for the joy of confident living.

I am thankful for those occasions that Christ has come to my immediate rescue in times of need. But there are many times, even now, that I simply cannot understand why something is happening. Yet, I have invested my trust in the coming of a Suffering Savior Who understands the scars and pains of life. I have found the faith to stand. And, so can you.

"So do not throw away your confidence; it will be richly rewarded. You need to persevere so that when you have done the will of God, you will receive what He has promised. For in just a very little while, He who is coming will come and will not delay" (Hebrews 10:35-37, NIV).

A Final Word

In a final word, I want to celebrate the joy and meaning God has restored to my life through the love and devotion of my wife, Vickie. She, too, has lived through the anguish of losing a companion and a partner in ministry. She has also emerged with a greater devotion to serve God and to fulfill His call on her life. The two of us are joyfully and fully committed to learn from the pain of the past as we move forward vigorously into the new challenges the Lord is opening for us day by day. "Being confident of this very thing, that He which hath begun a good work in you (us) will perform it until the day of Jesus Christ" Philippians 1:6 (KJV).

Together, Vickie and I encourage you to live daily, believing that God can do anything. Keep asking Him *'What is your Word for me in this situation?'* and, *'Lord, how do you want me to conduct myself in the midst of these circumstances?'*

Let frantic faith be replaced by a calm assurance that circumstances will not prevail; that the enemy will not succeed; that your uncertainties will not control you and the the promises of God will be certain! Even when the answers aren't enough and when you cannot understand, you can find the strength to stand in Christ!

None of us have all the answers, but, hopefully, we are more comfortable with the questions. The journey of confident living in Christ continues for us, and we pray it does for you also.

> "And I heard a loud voice from heaven saying, 'Behold, the tabernacle of God is with men, and He will dwell with them, and they shall be His people. God Himself will be with them and be their God. And God will wipe away every tear from their eyes; there shall be no more death, nor sorrow, nor crying. There shall be no more pain, for the former things have passed away. Then He who sat on the throne said, 'Behold, I make all things new.' And, He said to me, 'Write, for these words are true and faithful'" (Revelation 21:3-5, NKJV).

About the Author

Dr. R. Lamar Vest is one of today's most highly acclaimed ambassadors for Christianity. He has served a long and distinguished career leading some of the most prominent and productive ministries in evangelical faith. Many of the positions he has held would be considered peaks in a given ministry career, but for Vest each served as preparation for the next step in a remarkable ministry.

Called to preach at fifteen, he took his first pastorate at age 20 in South Carolina. He led two churches before becoming a state evangelist for the Church of God. In 1968, he began a sixteen-year period of leading state and denomination-wide youth programs. Within that period of time, he served as the Director of the International Youth and Christian Education Department for the Church of God.

In 1984, Vest was appointed as President of Lee College (now Lee University), the Church of God's flagship college. In two years, Vest reversed a downward trend of student enrollment and placed the Christian liberal arts college on a track to financial and academic stability.

After just two years at Lee, Vest was elected by his ministerial peers in the Church of God to the Executive Committee, the highest body of leaders in the denomination. Having served on this five-man leadership team for eight years, he advanced in 1990 to the top leadership post of General Overseer, where he would serve until his tenure limit in 1994. Just two years later, he was re-elected to the committee, advancing again to General Overseer in 2000 and served until 2004. Vest is one of the few ministers in the history of the Church of God to serve twice as General Overseer. He has served on the Church of God Council of Eighteen and has also been Director of Media Ministries.

Dr. Vest has been on the Executive Committee for United Bible Societies Global Board and served on the founding board of the Center for Spiritual Renewal. He was also Chairman of National Association of Evangelicals, one of the most influential cross-denominational, evangelical organizations.

Presently, he holds the position of President Emeritus of American Bible Society after having served as President for five years and a board member for seventeen years.

Dr. Vest is presently working with the Pentecostal Theological Seminary in Cleveland, TN as Adjunct Professor and as Director of the Center for Spiritual Leadership and Lifelong Learning. In addition, he continues to work as an Associate Pastor with the Times Square Church in New York City where he is pioneering a leadership development program involving several hundred pastors along with thousands of others worldwide.

Dr. Vest is a sought after international speaker in conferences and church conventions and has authored five books, numerous articles for print, and electronic media. He holds a Bachelor's degree from Lee University, a Master's degree from the Pentecostal Theological Seminary and a DLitt. from Lee University.

Made in the USA
Charleston, SC
31 May 2014